1982

ARISTOTLE'S THEORY
OF THE WILL

ARISTOTLE'S THEORY OF THE WILL

Anthony Kenny

New Haven
Yale University Press
1979

Library of Congress Cataloging in Publication Data

Kenny, Anthony John Patrick.
   Aristotle's theory of the will.
   Bibliography: p.
   Includes indexes.
   1. Aristotle—Ethics. 2. Ethics. 3. Free will
and determinism. 4. Will. I. Title.
B491.E7K47 1979   171'.3   79–426

   ISBN 0–300–02395–2

Printed in Great Britain

CONTENTS

INTRODUCTION

It is a commonplace of Aristotelian scholarship that Aristotle
had no theory of the will. Thus the most distinguished contemporary commentator on the *Nicomachean Ethics* can write
that in Aristotle's psychology the will does not occur at all: the
concept was invented only after eleven further centuries of
philosophical reflection.[1] No Aristotelian expression corresponds to the English expression 'freedom of the will'; Sir David
Ross thought that the best that could be said was that Aristotle
'shared the plain man's belief in free will but that he did not
examine the problem very thoroughly and did not express himself with perfect consistency'.[2]

This criticism of Aristotle depends on a certain view of the
nature of the will. According to a view familiar in modern philosophical tradition, the will is a phenomenon of introspective
consciousness. Volition is a mental event which precedes and
causes certain human actions: its presence or absence makes the
difference between voluntary actions. The freedom of the will
is to be located in the indeterminacy of these internal volitions.
The occurrence of volitions, and their freedom from causal
control, is a matter of intimate experience.

It is true that this account of the will is not to be found in
Aristotle. This is not to Aristotle's discredit, for this whole conception of volition and freedom has been subjected, in our own
time, to decisive criticism by philosophers such as Ryle and
Wittgenstein. Philosophers who accept the criticisms of this
school have attempted to build afresh a philosophical theory of

---

[1] R. -A. Gauthier, 1959, 218: 'dans la psychologie d'Aristote la volonté
n'existe pas'; 1970, 266: 'il a fallu aux hommes, après Aristote, quelque
onze siècles de reflexions pour inventer la volonté.'

[2] W. D. Ross, 1949, 211.

the springs of human action which will be free of the confusions
involved in the theory familiar in modern philosophical tradition. The resulting new structures bear a remarkable resem-
blance to what we find in Aristotle's *Ethics*.[1]

A satisfactory philosophical account of the will must relate
human action to ability, desire, and belief. It must therefore
contain three major elements, which may be combined in
different ways according to different theoretical assumptions:
it must contain a treatment of voluntariness, a treatment of
intentionality, and a treatment of rationality. In my view, the
treatment of voluntariness will have as its main thrust the exploration of the relationship between action and ability; the
treatment of intentionality will be mainly concerned to exhibit
the teleology of action and its relationship to desires and goals;
and the treatment of practical rationality will exhibit the
relationship between practical belief and action. But the
ability which enters into the definition of voluntariness cannot
be analysed without reference to the notion of desire; and the
relationship between belief and action cannot be presented
separately from the relationship between desire and action.
Thus the three elements constituting an account of the will
must necessarily be fused into a single whole if the account is
to make any pretence at adequacy.

In Aristotle's ethical treatises there is ample material relevant
to the study of voluntariness, the study of intentionality, and the
study of practical reasoning: effectively these treatises were the
starting point of systematic philosophical study of these topics,
and today they remain an abundant source of fresh insights into
the problems in the area. Aristotle's concepts do not coincide
exactly with those which a modern philosopher in the Anglo-
American tradition would employ: but in the case of voluntariness and practical reasoning his theoretical apparatus is close
enough to our own for the use of contemporary technical terms

---

[1] An influential treatment of problems of the will from a Wittgensteinian
standpoint was G. E. M. Anscombe's *Intention* (1957). I have tried to develop
my own philosophical account of these matters in *Action, Emotion and Will*
(1963) and *Will, Freedom and Power* (1975). Probably the currently most
influential theory of volition and action is that presented in numerous papers
by Donald Davidson. That theory too contains strongly Aristotelian features.

to be appropriate in reporting his views. In the case of intentionality matters are more complicated. Aristotle's discussion of προαίρεσις contains many elements which belong to the treatment of intentionality, but he has no technical concept which corresponds to our use of 'intention'. The three main elements to be presented in an account of Aristotle's theory of the will, therefore, are his account of voluntariness, his account of προαίρεσις, or purposive choice, and his account of practical reasoning. The three parts of the present book are devoted to these three topics.

In addition to its philosophical value, a study of Aristotle's treatment of the will is of great importance for those who are interested in the history of his ethical writings. Since the time of W. Jaeger early in the present century it has been the almost universal opinion of scholars that the *Nicomachean Ethics* represent Aristotle's mature thought and that the *Eudemian Ethics* date from a juvenile Platonising period. Opinions have differed about the third major ethical treatise in the corpus, the *Magna Moralia*: some regard it as post-Aristotelian, others as an authentic work predating the *Eudemian Ethics*. For many centuries it has been the practice of scholars to comment mainly on the *Nicomachean Ethics* and use the other treatises only to cast occasional light on difficult passages of that text. The question of the historical relationship between the treatises is complicated by the fact that in the manuscript tradition of the *Ethics* there are three books which make a double appearance, once as books four, five, and six of the *Eudemian Ethics*, and once as books five, six, and seven of the *Nicomachean Ethics*.

In a recent book I have argued that the scholarly consensus about the relationship between the ethical treatises is ill-founded.[1] On historical, stylistic, and philosophical grounds I have argued that the disputed books belonged originally with the *Eudemian Ethics* and not with the *Nicomachean*. Since these books are philosophically mature, and contain historical allusions suggesting a late date, the *Eudemian Ethics* should be assigned to the final period of Aristotle's activity, not to his apprenticeship. This leaves open the possibility that the *Magna Moralia*, which for the most part resembles the *Eudemian Ethics*

[1] *The Aristotelian Ethics*, 1978.

very closely in construction, may be a student's notes of the
Eudemian course. The exact chronological relationship between the Eudemian and Nicomachean treatises must await a
careful comparison between the texts taking account of the
Eudemian provenance of the disputed books.

The present book does not take for granted the historical
conclusions just presented: but it offers a contribution to the
comparison between the *Eudemian Ethics*, the *Nicomachean
Ethics* and the disputed books (which I shall henceforth call the
'*Aristotelian Ethics*').[1] The topics of the present study are discussed by Aristotle in all three contexts in a way which permits
a detailed comparison between them. The Nicomachean passages on the will have been the subject of detailed commentary
for centuries, and though there remain many problems about
their interpretation no scholar is likely to be able to produce
really fresh ideas about them. The only novelty that can be
claimed for the present treatment is that it takes the *Eudemian
Ethics* with equal seriousness and tries to resolve some of the
complexities in its much richer, but much less studied, chapters
on the will.

---

[1] Following the usage in Kenny, 1978, I shall abbreviate the titles to
'*NE*' '*EE*' and '*AE*'; books in the *NE* will be given arabic numerals, books
in the *EE* roman numerals, and books of the *AE* small capitals (thus *NE* 2,
EE II, *AE* B).

Part One

Voluntariness and Involuntariness

1. Human Agency in the Eudemian Ethics

The treatment of voluntariness in the *EE* marks a fresh start in that treatise. It is placed after the discussion of virtues as means, in the sixth chapter of book II. Despite the abruptness of the opening ('Let us take another starting-point') the treatment of voluntariness is more closely woven in to the theory of virtue in general in the *EE* than in the *NE*, where the opening of book 3 has only a punning reference to 'passion and action' to link the topic of voluntariness with that of virtue. The *EE* is also at pains to locate the theory of human action within a general theory of causation. It is principally to this task that II.6 is devoted.

The chapter is a difficult one to understand. An elaborate classification of types of cause and principle is drawn up: neither the exact lines of the classification nor the precise purpose of introducing it can be gathered without a close study of the text, and as the argument proceeds from proposition to proposition it is not always clear which is premise and which is conclusion. I will first set out the main lines of the discussion in the order given by Aristotle, and will then return to particular points of difficulty before trying to restructure the argument in more perspicuous manner.

All substances by nature are principles (ἀρχαί): for instance, living things beget their kind. Only man is also a principle of action or conduct (πρᾶξις). Principles which originate movement are controlling principles (κύριαι ἀρχαί). Principles which control necessary movements—God, perhaps—particularly deserve the name. Principles or axioms in mathematics are not controlling principles except in the sense that *if* the axioms were to change the theorems would change too. Man is a principle of movement, since actions are movements. All

principles are causes: a principle is an ultimate, or uncaused
cause (αἴτιον). Necessary effects have necessary causes, and
contingent effects have contingent causes. Men are controlling
principles and causes of contingent effects. We are praised and
blamed for things of which we are causes, not for things of
which necessity, nature, chance or other humans are causes.
Virtue and vice and the corresponding acts give rise to praise
and blame; therefore virtue and vice are concerned with the
acts of which we are causes and principles: and these by common consent are the acts which are voluntary and purposely
chosen. Since voluntariness is a broader category than purposive choice we must therefore study voluntariness.

Such are the main lines of the chapter: but many of its details
are obscure. The technical terms ἀρχή, κύριος, αἴτιος, ἐφ' αὐτῷ,
ἑκούσιον are introduced: it is not clear how they are related to
each other and how many are synonyms of each other. It is
unclear why the classification of ἀρχαί is undertaken at all. In
order to motivate the discussion of voluntariness within a treatise on virtue would it not be enough to introduce the final
considerations of the chapter? 'We are praised for virtue, we
are praised for what we are responsible for or cause (αἴτιος), we
cause voluntary actions, so let us investigate voluntariness.'
Why is anything more necessary?

The relation between the technical terms seems to be as
follows. Every principle is a cause, but not every cause is a
principle: only a cause whose causation has no further cause is a
principle. This is illustrated in the case of one of the types of
causation, namely the necessary causation characteristic of
geometry:

> Since if the angles of a triangle are equal to two right angles, it
> is necessary that the angles of a square are equal to four right
> angles, it is clear that the triangle's equalling two right angles
> is the cause of the square's equalling four right angles ... If
> there is no other cause of the triangle's having this property,
> this will be a principle as well as a cause of the consequential
> properties. (1222b32–37, 39–41)

Among first principles or ἀρχαί we can distinguish between

those which are causes of motion or change (κίνησις) and those which are not. Mathematical properties such as that illustrated in the above passage are clearly not causes of motion: but not all cases of physical causation are causation of motion either. The generation of one substance by another is a causation of subtance, not a causation of motion.¹ Causes which are causes of motion are called controlling causes, and principles which are principles of motion are called controlling principles.² Controlling principles in turn can be subdivided into those which control necessary movements and those which control contingent movements. God is the controlling cause of the necessary movements of the heavens; the contingent events of human affairs have contingent causes. Some of them are the results of human intervention and some of them are the results of chance. So we can draw up the following table, to illustrate the relationships between αἰτία, ἀρχή, and κύριος.³

¹ When a human being A is generated by another human being B, B has in his turn been generated by another human being C. How then can Aristotle call B an ἀρχή if an ἀρχή is to be an uncaused, originating cause? Doubtless the answer is that though B's existence was caused by C, B's generating of A is not caused by C. That is why above I wrote 'only a cause whose *causation* has no further cause is a principle'.

² Thus I interpret 1222b21 τῶν δ' ἀρχῶν ὅσαι τοιαῦται, ὅθεν πρῶτον αἱ κινήσεις, κύριαι λέγονται. ὅσαι τοιαῦται means 'those among principles which are like the human principles just mentioned in being the first origin of motions'. It is being an origin of motion, not being a *first* origin of motion, which makes something κύριος (cf. *AE* B.2, where it is explained that αἴσθησις is κυρία of action without being ἀρχή of action): something can control action without being the first controlling factor; the effect of being the *first* cause of motion is to make a cause not just κύριος but also ἀρχή. Many commentators and translators take κύριαι ἀρχαί to mean 'ἀρχαί properly so called'. This is a possible translation of the expression, though κυρίως ἀρχαί is the more usual Aristotelian expression for this sense; but in the present context it is unlikely to be the sense, since the κύριαι ἀρχαί of 22a21 are clearly meant to link up with man's being ἀρχὴ καὶ κύριος at 23a3, and there the only possible sense is the one just explained.

³ The table does not include, nor does Aristotle's text here tell us where to include, the natural, non-voluntary motions of human beings. Should φύσις appear with God as a cause of necessary movement, as well as generation? Or do these count as contingent movements, and should those brought about by man be divided into those brought about by man by nature and those brought about by him by choice? See pp. 8, 58.

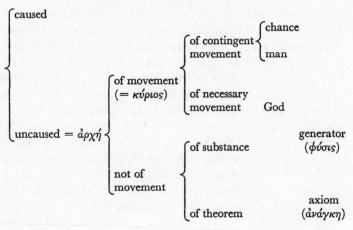

There follows a very difficult passage, whose sections I shall number for ease of reference. I translate as literally as may be.

(1) So if there are some of the things that are that admit of being otherwise, it is necessary that their principles be likewise. For what results from necessary things is itself necessary, but things from thence admit of becoming the opposite. (2) What depends on men themselves is, a great deal, of this kind of thing, and they themselves are the principles of things of this kind. (3) So, of the actions of which man is principle and controller—of those at least of which he is in control of whether they occur or not—it is clear that they admit of occurring or not, and that it depends on him whether they occur or not. (4) But of what it depends on him to do or not to do, he is himself the cause; and what he is the cause of depends on him. (1222b41–3a9)

The first section is the least problematic: the reference to 'the things' (τὰ ὄντα) which admit of being otherwise clearly, from the context, concerns not merely substantial things, but any properties which may be present or absent, any events which may or may not occur, actions which may or may not be performed. When Aristotle says that their principles 'must be likewise' he does not mean that the principles must themselves be contingent beings. That is in fact the case—human beings who perform contingent actions are contingent beings who are born and die—but Aristotle's point here is that the principle of a contingent effect must have a particular contingency corresponding to the contingency of the effect. What that is, in the case of actions, he goes on to make clear in the succeeding sections.[1]

The Greek of the first sentence of section 2 has an awkward ambiguity which it is impossible entirely to reproduce in English. ὃ ἐφ' αὑτοῖς ἐστι τοῖς ἀνθρώποις, πολλὰ τῶν τοιούτων may mean either 'What depends on men themselves is—a great deal of it—of this kind' or 'What depends on men themselves is a great deal of this kind of thing'.[2] Either reading sets a problem: if we read the sentence in the first way we have to ask ourselves what are the things which depend on men which are not contingent; if we read it in the second way we have to inquire which are the contingent matters which do not depend on man. Either reading, it seems to me, is an expression of something which Aristotle believed: some things depend on men, in the sense of being within the competence of human nature, without being contingent in the sense of avoidable; and some things are contingent without being the results of human intervention: e.g. matters of luck. As Aristotle goes on to mention the possibility of luck a few lines further on, the second reading seems to me to be the more appropriate one in the context. But it is worth while spending some time on the proposition expressed by the first reading of the sentence, since what it enunciates is crucial for an understanding of the Eudemian doctrine of things that 'depend on us', are 'in our power', are ἐφ' ἡμῖν.

In *NE* 3 we are told that where it is in our power to do something, it also in our power not to do it, and when the 'no' is in

---

[1] 'From thence', however it is to be literally construed (see von Fragstein, 1967, 122), clearly refers to contingent principles.

[2] Because the plural πολλά comes awkwardly after the singular ὅ, Fritzsche who took the first reading ('multaque, quae penes homines sunt, eiusmodi sunt') emended ὅ to ἅ. Dirlmeier takes the first reading, without emendation, arguing implausibly that the reliable good behaviour of the virtuous man is something necessary, not contingent (1969, 270). Von Fragstein argues well for the interpretation I have accepted: 'was den Menschen in ihre Verfügung gegeben ist, ist ein Grossteil des erwähnten Bereiches des So-und-anders' (1967, 122).

B

our power the 'yes' is also (1113b7–8). If this were also the doctrine of the *EE*, then it would indeed be impossible for there to
be a class of actions that were within men's power to do but
which were not humanly avoidable. But the use of ἐφ᾽ ἡμῖν in
the *EE*, and in the *AE*, seems to differ in this respect from that
in the *NE*, and it repays closer examination.

EE II.8 makes clear that there are some actions which human
beings do which are not in their power to do, in the sense that
they are not the results of their natural capacities:

> What is not the result of a man's own natural desire and
> reasoning is not in his own power. For this reason, those who
> are rapt and who prophesy, though what they produce is a
> product of thought, we do not say that it is in their power to
> say what they say or do what they do. (1224a25–33)

It seems to be the demands of the particular context which
restrict to desire and reasoning the natural capacities whose
exercise counts as something in our power: for at *AE* A.8 we
read this:

> What is done without knowledge, or with knowledge but not
> in our power or under coercion, is involuntary. For there are
> many natural processes that we perform (πράττομεν) or under-
> go in full knowledge, none of which is either voluntary or in-
> voluntary, for example, growing old or dying. (1135a34ff)

Now if growing old was something which was not ἐφ᾽ ἡμῖν, not in
our power, then it would by the definition given be involuntary
rather than non-voluntary: it would be something done 'with
knowledge but not in our power'. The 'for' introducing the
second sentence is in fact meant to explain why the addition of
'not in our power' was necessary and why voluntariness cannot
be defined in terms of knowledge alone. Since growing old is
something that we can do, but not something that we can avoid
doing, this passage of the *AE* is inconsistent with the statement
of the *NE* that wherever doing something is in our power, then
not doing the same thing is also in our power.[1] In the *EE* dis-

---

[1] Thus the *NE* says that being hungry is not something which is ἐφ᾽ ἡμῖν
(1113b27).

cussion of voluntariness, however, at 1224b34, notice is explicitly taken of these natural processes such as 'growing grey and growing old and suchlike'. Dying and growing old are natural processes which are necessary and unavoidable: they therefore are examples of the kinds of things which we do, and which are in our power to do, but are not 'things which admit of occurring and not occurring'. It is for this reason that the *EE*, unlike the *NE*, when it wants to demarcate the class of actions that are voluntary or choosable, does so by speaking not simply of those things which it is in our power to do, but those things which it is in our power to do *or not to do*.[1] The addition would be superfluous for the *NE*, in the light of 1113b7–8; it has a job to do in the *EE*.

The third section follows awkwardly on the second, and the exact logical link between the two is not clear. Having been told that the principles of contingent things are contingent, and that men are principles of contingent things, we expect the conclusion to be drawn that men are themselves contingent agents. Instead, what seems to be drawn as a conclusion is that human actions are contingent; something which seems already to have been stated in the previous section. In the whole argument it is not obvious what are premises and what are conclusions.

The unclarity is the result of the excessive compression, and it is best removed by a rather voluminous paraphrase. The thought proceeds as follows. In general contingent effects have similar ἀρχαί. There are contingent things in men's power, and the effects of the exercise of human power have men as their ἀρχαί. Therefore, men are, in a sense which we must immediately go on to make precise, contingent ἀρχαί. Since actions are κινήσεις, and since the ἀρχή of a κίνησις is κύριος, wherever a man is an ἀρχή of a πρᾶξις he is also κύριος of it. In some cases in which a man is ἀρχή and κύριος of a πρᾶξις he is ἀρχή and κύριος of its occurring or not occurring: this is the precise sense in which men are contingent ἀρχαί.[2] In such cases it is not enough that

[1] Compare *EE* 1225a19, 1225b8, 1225b36, 1226a28, 1228a5 etc. with *NE* 1111a23, 1113a11, 1113b21, 1113b26.
[2] The parallel passage of the *MM* says that it is προαίρεσις which is the ἀρχή of action (as the seed is an ἀρχή of a new tree) (1187a33,b15). In the light of the passage discussing prohairesis in *AE* B.2 (ὀρεκτικὸς νοῦς ἢ

the effect should be contingent in the sense of admitting of contrary properties: it must be contingent in the sense of being capable of occurring or not occurring.¹ (Growing old is an instance of a πρᾶξις which is contingent in the broad sense but not the narrow sense: I cannot help growing old, but it depends on me whether I grow old sourly or gracefully.) Not only must the effect have this radical contingency: if I am to be κύριος of its occurring or not occurring, then it must depend *on me* which of the two possible contingencies occurs. (Growing grey is contingent in the radical sense: I may or may not grow grey. But which of the contingencies is realised does not, alas, depend on me.) Thus understood, the argument proceeds without repetition or circularity, but with a large number of tacit premises which need to be provided from the context.

The fourth section presents less difficulty, but is not without ambiguity. Since, if you do something which is in your power, you are an ἀρχή of it (from 1223a3), and since every ἀρχή is an αἴτιος (from 1222b30), we can conclude *a fortiori* that, as the first clause of (4) tells us, man is the cause of what it is in his power to do or not to do. But when we are told, conversely, that 'what he is the cause of is in his power' are we to take 'is in his power' in the broad sense or as being an abbreviation for 'is in his power to do or not to do'? The preceding context would suggest that we take it in the broad sense: for in the cases where a man is an ἀρχή, but not κύριος τοῦ εἶναι καὶ μὴ εἶναι, he will be an αἴτιος without its being in his power to do or not to do the action. But whichever view we take, we are brought up short by the paragraph which ends the chapter:

It is clear that virtue and vice have to do with matters where the man himself is the cause and principle of his actions. We

---

προαίρεσις . . . καὶ ἡ τοιαύτη ἀρχὴ ἄνθρωπος, 1139b5) this does not conflict with the *EE*: it is man *qua* chooser who is ἀρχὴ πράξεως in the strictest sense. But whereas a tree can produce seeds for only one kind of tree, man produces προαίρεσις for many kinds of action. There are however, according to *MM* and *EE*, voluntary but unchosen actions.

¹ The distinction is between being ἐνδεχόμενον ἐναντίως ἔχειν (b41) and being ἐνδεχόμενον γίγνεσθαι καὶ μή (a5ff). The distinction is preserved in Solomon's translation as between that which 'may have the opposite to its actual qualities' and that which 'may either happen or not happen'.

must then ascertain of what actions he is the cause and principle. Now we all agree that each man is the cause of voluntary things done in accordance with his own choice, but that he is not the cause of involuntary things. (1223a15–19)

This paragraph does indeed leave it open to us to say that man is an αἴτιος of natural processes like growing old, since these are neither voluntary nor involuntary according to *AE* A.8, 1135b1. But since one class of involuntary actions is actions done in error, there will be some cases even within the narrow class of actions-in-our-power-to-do-or-not-to-do of which we will not count as the cause.

So far as I can see, the only way to render this passage consistent with what goes before is to take Aristotle to be using αἴτιος first in a broad sense corresponding to the translation 'cause', and then in a narrow sense corresponding to the word 'responsible'. Up to 1223a9 he is using αἴτιος in such a way that any ἀρχή of any kind is αἴτιον of whatever in any way takes its origin from it; in 1223a15 he uses it so that not all the actions that human beings do, and not all the actions that are in their power to do, and not even all the actions that are in their power to do or not to do, are actions of which they are αἴτιοι; but only that sub-class of actions in one's power to do and not to do

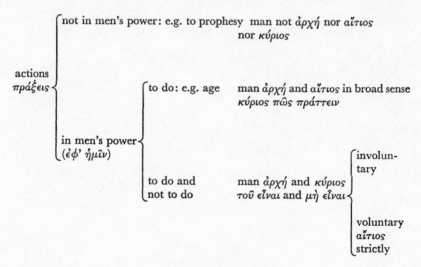

which are voluntary (i.e. performed in full knowledge of the circumstances, as we learn at 1225b1ff after considerable further discussion). If we allow Aristotle this confusingly equivocal terminology, we thus obtain the following coherent and intelligible classification of things that human beings do (see p. 11). Chapter 7 proceeds to discuss how the class of actions which are in our power to do and not to do are to be subdivided into voluntary and involuntary ones: and to that we now turn.

2. *Voluntariness and Desire in the* Eudemian Ethics

Chapter 7 discusses how the class of actions which are in our power to do or not to do can be subdivided into those which are voluntary and those which are involuntary. The basic principle of the investigation is the reasonable hypothesis that the difference between voluntary and involuntary actions within the broad class is a matter of their relation to the mental state of the agent. Is there a mental state such that being in accordance with it can be identified with voluntariness, and being in conflict with it can be identified with involuntariness? Mental states are either cognitive or affective or mixtures of both: so Aristotle explores in turn the possibility of identifying the voluntary/involuntary distinction with the relationship to some affective state (ὄρεξις being his most general term for these states), with the relationship to some cognitive state (διάνοια being his most general term here) and with the relationship to the state of προαίρεσις, which, as he later explains to us, is a combination of both cognition and desire (1227a4).

The affective states coming under the rubric of ὄρεξις can be grouped into three: βούλησις (volition) θυμός (anger) and ἐπιθυμία (sensual desire and appetite). These are the three types of desire corresponding to the Platonic tripartite soul of reason, temper, and appetite. Thus we have the following divisions:

$$
\begin{cases}
\text{ὄρεξις} \\
\text{(desire)} \\
\text{διάνοια} \\
\text{(cognition—contrasted with ἄγνοια)} \\
\text{προαίρεσις} \\
\text{(provisionally treated as co-ordinate to desire and cognition)}
\end{cases}
\begin{cases}
\text{βούλησις (desire of λόγος} = \text{volition)} \\
\text{θυμός (desire of temper} = \text{anger)} \\
\text{ἐπιθυμία (desire of appetite} = \text{lust, etc)}
\end{cases}
$$

First, then, can voluntariness be identified with being in accordance with appetite, and involuntariness with being against appetite? Aristotle appears to offer two arguments for the identification and two arguments against it. For the identification: (1) What conflicts with appetite is painful, what is painful is involuntary, so what is in accord with appetite is voluntary. (2) The incontinent man acts unjustly, and so involuntarily; but the only thing he is acting in accordance with is appetite; so acting in accordance with appetite is voluntary. Against the identification: (3) The incontinent man acts in accordance with appetite, so if we accept the identification he acts voluntarily. But he is acting against what he knows to be best, and no one wills to do this; so he is acting against his will, and therefore involuntarily. So accepting the identification would lead to the absurd conclusion that a man can act both voluntarily and involuntarily. (4) The continent man acts justly, and so voluntarily; but he is acting against appetite. So if acting against appetite is identified with acting involuntarily, we again have the absurd result of an action both voluntary and involuntary (1223a29–b17).

Set out thus in their bare bones, the arguments may seem plausible. Examined closely, they are very strange indeed.[1] Each of them contains either obviously invalid moves, or premises which we know Aristotle would reject. Oddest of all, Aristotle, having simply set out the arguments for and against the identification without apparently adjudicating between them, seems to proceed immediately as if it had been established that the identification was impossible.

Set out in full the first argument for the identification runs as follows:

> Now all that is in agreement with appetite would seem to be voluntary; for all the involuntary seems to be forced, and what is forced is painful, and so is all that men do and suffer from compulsion—as Evenus says, 'all to which we are compelled is unpleasant'. So that if an act is painful it is forced on us, and if forced it is painful. But all that is contrary to ap-

---

[1] In what follows, I am much indebted to an unpublished discussion by Mr J. O. Urmson.

petite is painful—for appetite is for the pleasant—and therefore forced and involuntary; what then agrees with appetite
is voluntary; for these two are opposites. (1223a29–36,
trans. Solomon)

The steps of the argument, then, are these:

(1) For all *x*, if *x* is involuntary *x* is forced

(2) For all *x*, if *x* is forced *x* is painful

So   (3) For all *x*, *x* is forced if and only if *x* is painful

(4) For all *x*, if *x* is contrary to appetite, *x* is painful

So   (5) For all *x*, if *x* is contrary to appetite, *x* is forced

And (6) For all *x*, if *x* is contrary to appetite, *x* is involuntary

But (7) Being contrary to appetite is the opposite of being in
accord with appetite

So   (8) For all *x*, if *x* is in accord with appetite, *x* is voluntary.

The difficulties here are many. (1) is not a proposition which
Aristotle accepts: involuntary actions need not be cases of
force, they may be cases of error (1225b6). The biconditional
(3) does not follow from the conditional (2) (whether in its prose
or its verse form); nor would Aristotle accept it, since as we
shall see, he has a technical concept of 'continence' (ἐγκράτεια):
the continent man's struggle with his desires is painful but not
forced (1224b15). (5) follows from (3) and (4), indeed, though
again it is a proposition to which Aristotle would regard the
continent man as providing a counter-example; but (6) does not
follow from any of the previous propositions, since (1) is a one-
way conditional and not a biconditional. From (6) and (7), by
double negation and contraposition, we would obtain not (8)
but 'For all *x*, if *x* is voluntary, *x* is in accord with appetite'; but
perhaps Aristotle is tacitly appealing to some more complicated
principle according to which truth is preserved if opposites are
systematically substituted for opposites throughout a proposition. In any case, it is unclear whether Aristotle was working
for the conclusion (8) or for the stronger conclusion

16 *Aristotle's Theory of the Will*

(8a) For all *x*, *x* is in accord with appetite if *x* is voluntary

The wording of this argument itself suggests that (8); the wider context treats it as an argument for (8a).

The second argument for the identification runs thus:

> Further, all wickedness makes one more unjust, and incontinence seems to be wickedness, the incontinent being the sort of man that acts in accordance with his appetite and contrary to his reason, and shows his incontinence when he acts in accordance with his appetite; but to act unjustly is voluntary, so that the incontinent will act unjustly by acting according to his appetite; he will then act voluntarily, and what is done according to appetite is voluntary. (1223a36–b3)

We may try to set out the steps here as follows:[1]

(1) For all *x*, if *x* is wicked *x* is unjust

(2) For all *x*, if *x* is incontinent, *x* is wicked

(3) For all *x*, *x* is incontinent if *x* obeys appetite against reason

(4) For all *x*, if *x* is injust, *x* is voluntary

So (5) For all *x*, if *x* is incontinent, *x* is voluntary (acts voluntarily)

And (6) For all *x*, if *x* obeys appetite, *x* is voluntary (acts voluntarily).

We meet the same sorts of difficulties here as in the first argument. (1) is a proposition which Aristotle might have accepted, provided that injustice is taken as the general injustice described in *AE* A.1 (1131a8–10); but (2) seems in flat contradiction to the whole drive of *AE* c which is to draw a distinction between the incontinent man and the really wicked man.[2] The present

---

[1] Aristotle sometimes speaks of the attributes of the incontinent man, and sometimes of those of incontinent action. For simplicity's sake the formalisation here ignores this, using so far as possible propositions which would apply to either case.

[2] ἀκρασία is systematically distinguished from κακία (1145a16) and we are told that the ἀκρατής is not πονηρός but only ἡμιπόνηρος. ἀκρασία and μοχθηρία are distinguished at 1148b2, 1149a16, 1150b32.

passage is the first introduction of the incontinent man in the context of the *Eudemian Ethics*: the definition of him and his action in (3) fits well enough the account of incontinence elsewhere in the *EE* and *AE*; but (3) is not what is needed in order to derive (6), but something like

(3a) For all *x*, if *x* obeys appetite, *x* is incontinent.

(4) presents no difficulty, and fits the account in *AE* A.8 of the voluntariness of injustice (1135b17ff). But as it stands, even if we accept all the premises, the argument does not yield an identification of voluntariness with obedience to appetite: it does not even yield the conclusion that whatever accords with appetite is voluntary, since the possibility is left open that activity in accordance with reason as well as with appetite is not voluntary. Perhaps Aristotle thought this to be sufficiently implausible for him to assume its contrary. The main thrust of the argument is undoubtedly that if voluntariness is to be identified with being in accord with some mental state, then the voluntariness of incontinent action has to be identified with its accordance with appetite, since that is the only mental state that it accords with; and that is enough to show that accordance with appetite is sufficient for voluntariness. It will not show that it is necessary for voluntariness; but then Aristotle does not, at this stage, say that it does (1223b4): 'From these considerations,' he says, 'what is done in accordance with appetite would seem voluntary.' He now goes on to offer arguments to show 'the opposite'. What does he regard as the opposite of the proposition that whatever accords with appetite is voluntary? The first argument offered is an argument to prove the contradictory of the proposition: *viz.*, that not everything that accords with appetite is voluntary. The second argument offers a proof of a rather different proposition: *viz.*, that not everything that discords with appetite is involuntary. The thesis 'that whatever accords with appetite is voluntary and that whatever discords with appetite is involuntary' seems clearly to be conceived as a single target, a single identification thesis to be argued against.

The first argument against the identification thesis runs thus:

What a man does voluntarily, he does in accordance with his

will; and what he does in accordance with his will, he does voluntarily. Now no one wills what he thinks to be bad. But a man acting incontinently does not do what he wills; for to act incontinently is to act through appetite contrary to what one thinks best. The upshot will be that the same person will act at the same time voluntarily and involuntarily; and this is impossible.

Simplifying and formalising again, we obtain:

(1) For all x, x acts voluntarily if x does what he wills

(2) For all x, if x does what he thinks bad, it is not the case that x does what he wills

(3) For all x, if x acts incontinently, he does what he thinks bad

So (4) For all x, if x acts incontinently, x does not do what he wills

So (5) For all x, if x acts incontinently, x does not act voluntarily

(6) For all x, if x acts incontinently, x acts in accord with appetite

(7) For all x, if x acts in accord with appetite, x acts voluntarily

So (8) For all x, if x acts incontinently, x acts voluntarily

So (9) For all x, if x acts incontinently, x acts voluntarily and involuntarily

(10) For some x, x acts incontinently

So (11) For some x, x acts voluntarily and involuntarily

So (12) (= Not-7), It is not the case that for all x, if x acts in accord with appetite, x acts voluntarily.

Here, at last, we have a valid argument: an unusually explicitly formulated *reductio ad absurdum*,[1] the only premises left

---

[1] Not, of course, an instance of RAA in the technical sense of natural deduction systems of propositional calculus: (11) is not in the form p and not-p. 11 (or the more precise version of it at 1223b25) is absurd *ex vi termini* ἑκών.

tacit being the premise to be reduced (7), which is easily sup-
plied from the context and the conclusion; plus the assumption
that incontinence occurs. (4) follows from (2) and (3), and (5)
from (1) and (4), which gives us one half of (4); (8) follows from
(6) and (7), and (9) from (5) and (8); and (9) plus (10) gives us
the absurdity (11). What is bizarre about the argument is the
first premise. In the first place, it already by itself amounts to a
contradiction of the conclusion of the previous argument, unless
we take βούλησις and ἐπιθυμία to be coextensive; in the second
place, it expresses a proposition which Aristotle clearly did not
accept, and which only twenty four lines later (1223b29) he
treats as being still a wide-open question. The *reductio*, of course,
shows only that the premises cannot all be consistently held, it
does not show which of them to reject: one way of avoiding it
would be to reject the possibility of incontinence; another, more
in accord with general Aristotelian theory, would be to take the
argument as showing the falsity of the first premise itself.

The second argument against the identification is, like the
first, a valid *reductio* based on some surprisingly unAristotelian
premises:

A continent man will act justly, and more so than incontinence; for continence is a virtue and virtue makes men more
just. Now a man acts continently when he acts against appetite in accordance with reason. So that if to act justly is
voluntary as to act unjustly is—for both these seem to be
voluntary, and if the one is, so must the other be—and if to
act contrary to appetite is involuntary, then the same man
will at the same time do the same thing voluntarily and
involuntarily. (1223b10–17)

We may formalise thus:

    (1) For all x, if x is continent, x is virtuous

    (2) For all x, if x is virtuous, x is just

So (3) For all x, if x is continent, x is just

    (4) For all x, if x is continent action, x is in conflict with
        appetite

(5) For all x, if x is just action x is voluntary action

(6) For all x, if x is in conflict with appetite, x is involuntary

(7) For some x, x is continent action

So   (8) For some x, is both voluntary and involuntary action.

Here, as in the second argument for the identification, Aristotle slips easily from talking about a certain kind of person (the continent) to talking about a certain kind of state (continence) and a certain kind of action (continent action). Steps (1) to (3) above have accordingly been stated in a way which allows them to be true both of the kind of person and of the kind of action. This enables the argument to be set out in a way which is formally valid. (3) follows from (1) and (2); from (3) and (5) it follows that continent action is voluntary action, and from (4) and (6) that continent action is involuntary action; so if we assume (7), which is not explicitly formulated in Aristotle's text, we obtain (8) which is absurd given that 'voluntary' and 'involuntary' are contraries. The *reductio* leaves it open which premise we are to withdraw: Aristotle treats it as a disproof of (6), the second half of the identification thesis. Premises (2), (4), (5) and (7) are all acceptable Aristotelian doctrines: but (1) is in conflict not only with the teaching of *AE* c on continence but also with the statement in II.11 that virtue and continence are two different things (1227b16).

Aristotle now goes on to say that the same arguments can be used for and against the identification of voluntary action with action in accordance with temper (θυμός) (1223b18–27). For the two features of appetite on which the arguments turned were these: acting against it is painful, and it is the subject matter of continence and incontinence. But to fight against temper is equally painful; and there is incontinence of temper no less than incontinence of appetite.[1] Hence, one can simply rewrite the arguments, replacing 'appetite' with 'temper' and

[1] *Pace* Walzer (1929, 105) this is in perfect accord with *AE* c.6; in both *AE* c and *EE* 2 ἀκρασία, if not expressly qualified, is taken to be concerned with appetite; in both the conflict between reason and the less rational parts of the soul is exemplified in each kind of ἀκρασία.

'incontinent of temper' for 'incontinent' *sans phrase*. I shall not attempt to spell this out: Aristotle was no doubt wise in thinking this an exercise best left to the reader. Aristotle concludes (1223b25–26) that if we are to identify voluntariness with concordance with ὄρεξις, volition is a more promising candidate for the appropriate ὄρεξις than either appetite or temper.

There is no doubt that the arguments we have just been considering are extremely unsatisfactory if taken as representing Aristotle's own position. Each one of them contains either premises which we know he rejected, or deductive fallacies which he should have detected. No doubt matters can be patched up with a little charitable emendation.[1] But emendation is uncalled for: the difficulties dwindle when we realise that Aristotle is not here arguing in his own person but reporting arguments of others.

This interpretation of the text is most strongly suggested by a comparison with the parallel passage in the *Magna Moralia*. There, in chapters 12 and 13 of book 1, the same arguments appear,[2] followed by a consideration of the proposal to identify voluntariness by reference to the will (which we shall consider shortly in its Eudemian context). We are then told: 'Since, then, certain arguments appear to conflict with each other, we must discuss voluntariness with greater precision' (1188b36–37). It is in accordance with Aristotle's general method first to set out ἀπόριαι arising from the views of the many and the wise on a given topic, and then to offer his own account of the matter in a way which preserves so far as possible the element of truth in the

---

[1] Thus Urmson has considered emending λυπηρὸν καί at 1223a29–30 to ἀκούσιον καὶ λυπηρόν; Allan has proposed καὶ γὰρ μᾶλλον τῆς ἀκρασίας ἡ ἐγκράτεια ἀρετή at 1223b11 in place of καὶ μᾶλλον τῆς ἀκρασίας. ἡ γὰρ ἐγκράτεια ἀρετή. The parallel with the description of ἀκρασία as μοχθηρία at 1223a37 seems to me to tell against Allan's proposal.

[2] The order of the arguments is varied. Whereas the *EE* sets out first two arguments for the identification (the pain and pleasure argument and the injustice of incontinence argument) and then two arguments against it (the argument that no one wills evil and the argument from the justice of continence), the *MM* sets out two pairs of conflicting arguments by reversing the order of incontinence-is-unjust and no-one-wills-evil. Moreover the *MM* presents the contrasting conclusions as 'action in accord with appetite is voluntary' and 'action in accord with appetite is involuntary'.

opinions which gave rise to the problem but setting it out
with greater precision (cf. *EE* 1.6, 1216b26–1217a20; *AE* c,
1146b6–8).

The Eudemian passage itself offers indications enough of its
dialectical nature. It is peppered with Aristotle's favourite expressions for reporting the views and arguments of others without committing himself to them (δοκεῖ 1223a30, 37, 1223b15,
19; δόξειε 1223a29, b4). The presence in the arguments of
doctrines clearly rejected in the same book of the *EE* should
make us wary of assuming that Aristotle endorsed the validity
of the arguments any more than the truth of the premises.

But if the arguments are recognised by Aristotle to be flawed
and inadequate, why does he go on at 1223b29 to talk as if the
possibility of defining voluntariness in terms of appetite and
temper had been excluded, and again, after excluding a
definition in terms of will, to state that it is now obvious that
voluntariness is not acting in accordance with any kind of
desire (1223b37)? The answer is to be found in an examination
of the passage linking the dialectical arguments we have just
considered with the argument to show that voluntariness cannot be defined in terms of will.

> [From these arguments it would follow that] acting in
> accordance with will has more claim to be voluntary than
> acting in accordance with appetite and temper. A proof of
> this is that we do many things voluntarily without anger or
> appetite.[1] It remains then to consider whether what is willed
> and what is voluntary are the same thing. This too seems
> impossible. For it is an assumption of ours and it is commonly
> admitted that wickedness makes men more unjust . . .
> (1223b25–30)

This passage makes clear that Aristotle thinks that quite inde-
pendently of the arguments he has just patiently rehearsed he
has a proof that voluntariness is not in accord with temper or
appetite: the simple and obvious fact that we often act voluntarily without being in a state of passion. This is a more general,
though less striking, phenomenon than that which provided the

---

[1] τεκμήριον δέ· πολλὰ γὰρ πράττομεν ἑκόντες ἄνευ ὀργῆς καὶ ἐπιθυμίας.
For the slightly puzzling construction compare, e.g., *Pol.* 7.16, 1335a15.

basis for the dialectical arguments: namely, the phenomenon of
conflict between passion and action. It is this brief but adequate
argument, and not the dubious dialectical ones, which entitles
him to conclude that voluntariness cannot be defined in terms
of temper or appetite.[1]

The subsequent argument to exclude a definition of voluntariness in terms of volition is, unlike the previous ones, intended by
Aristotle to be convincing.[2] It begins not just 'it seems' or 'it is
commonly admitted' (δοκεῖ) but 'it is an assumption of ours'
(ὑπόκειται γὰρ ἡμῖν). It proceeds thus:

> It is an assumption of ours, and it is commonly admitted, that
> wickedness makes men more unjust, and incontinence seems
> to be wickedness of a sort. But the opposite will result (*sc.*
> from the hypothesis that voluntariness is action in accord-
> ance with will). For no one wills what he thinks bad, but
> when he becomes incontinent he does what he thinks bad. If
> then unjust action is voluntary, and what is voluntary is what
> is in accord with willing, when a man becomes incontinent
> he will no longer be committing injustice, but he will be more
> just than before he became incontinent. But this is impossible.
> (1223b30–36)

[1] Why are the dialectical arguments spelt out at all if Aristotle is going to
produce a different and brisker argument for their conclusion? The answer
is that they set the stage for the discussion of the question whether continence
and incontinence are cases of voluntariness or cases of force which takes up
most of II.8. The erroneous dictum that whatever is involuntary is forced is
taken up at 1224a11, and the argument from pleasure and pain is des-
patched at 1224b15; the rest of the section is devoted to showing that cases
of conflict between two natural springs of action, such as occurs in continence and incontinence, are not cases of force, but cases of voluntariness.
It is this which shows that the occurrence of continence and incontinence
prevents the identification of voluntariness with any *one* form of ὄρεξις;
which was the main burden, however clumsily argued, of the dialectical
arguments. Thus the solution of the ἀπορία preserves the truth in the ἔνδοξα.
Again the comparison with the *MM* is instructive. The *MM* does not have
a section corresponding to the first part of II.8; instead, the dialectical
arguments have themselves been modified so that they accord better with
Aristotelian theory: thus incontinence is not called wickedness, nor is
continence called a virtue; it is merely described as a subject-matter for
praise (1188a19) (cf. *EE* 1227b).

[2] It is referred back to as a convincing proof (δέδεικται) at 1224a2).

C

If we formalise along the following lines, we can build a *reductio ad absurdum*:

(1) For all *x*, if *x* is incontinent *x* is unjust

(2) For all *x*, if *x* is unjust action *x* is voluntary action

(3) For all *x*, if *x* is incontinent action *x* is action thought bad

(4) For all *x*, if *x* is action thought bad *x* is action not willed

(5) For all *x*, if *x* is voluntary action *x* is willed action

So (6) For all *x*, if *x* is incontinent action *x* is not unjust action.

(6) does indeed follow from (2) to (5), *via* two moves of *modus ponendo ponens* and two of *modus tollendo tollens;* and on the assumption that incontinence occurs (6) is incompatible with the assumption (1). (5) is rejected as the least certain of the premises leading to the *reductio:* certainly, this time, all the others are propositions which we know Aristotle himself accepted.[1]

Having ruled out each of the three forms of desire, appetite temper and will, Aristotle concludes that voluntariness cannot be defined as accord with desire. It is sometimes objected that he should have considered the possibility that voluntariness con-

---

[1] In order to establish (1) Aristotle makes a detour through μοχθηρία; but the step is expressed more cautiously here than in the dialectical arguments. ἀκρασία is only μοχθηρία τις: something which is compatible with the distinction between ἀκρασία and real μοχθηρία in *AE* c. The only puzzling feature of the argument is the form in which Aristotle expresses the proposition formalised as (6). 'When a man becomes incontinent he will no longer be committing injustice, but he will be more just than before he became incontinent.' One can see that on the basis of the argument his action will not be unjust, because not voluntary: but how will this make him *more* just? That must depend on what he was doing *before* he became incontinent, surely; if he was then leading a blameless life, then we should not say he is *more* just through involuntary incontinence; if he was previously a vicious man, whose will has been converted but who cannot yet live up to his new principles, then what is absurd in saying that incontinence *has* made him more just? It is at least a step up towards justice from remorsefree wrongdoing.

sisted in agreement with one or other kind of desire: in agreement either with appetite, or with temper, or with volition. But what Aristotle has been considering is the possibility that the voluntary/involuntary distinction could be identified with the distinction between acting in accord with desire and acting in conflict with desire; and while he might accept that action in accord with any one of the three kinds of the desire is voluntary,[1] he certainly could not accept that action in conflict with any one of the three kinds of desire is involuntary (for the actions of the continent and incontinent furnish counterexamples).

προαίρεσις, or purposive choice, can also be ruled out as furnishing a definition of voluntariness. We have just seen that not everything that is voluntary is something that is willed. But further, not everything that is willed is purposely chosen, for we do some things on a sudden volition, without the deliberation which we shall later be told (ii.10) is characteristic of purposive choice. προαίρεσις is therefore at two removes from voluntariness.

So Aristotle sums up:

If, as we saw, the voluntary must be one of these three—action in accordance with desire, with choice, or with cognition—and two of these have been ruled out, the remaining alternative is that voluntary action is action performed in a certain state of cognition. (1224a5–8)

We must remember that the discussion has long reached the point at which it has been made clear that voluntary actions are a sub-class of actions which are in our power to do or not to do. At this point, Aristotle tells us that the subdivision is to be made by taking into account the cognitive state of the agent. He will explain in detail how this is to be done later (at 11224b37ff, and, if *AE* belongs with *EE*, in *AE* a.8), but before doing so he interpolates a treatment of the topic of βία or force, paying particular attention to the case of the incontinent.

Since the time of Socrates, the case of incontinence had been

---

[1] Aristotle could not agree to this without qualification; action in error might be in accord with desire, but involuntary because of the error.

a test-case for theories of voluntariness. In the *NE*, as we shall see, Aristotle regards the two great categories of involuntariness as being force and error. In *EE* II Aristotle discusses whether the incontinent man can be said to act under force; in *AE* c he discusses whether the incontinent man can be said to act in error. The two passages taken together add up to his solution to the problem whether a man can do wrong voluntarily.

3. Force and Involuntariness in the Nicomachean Ethics

The first chapters of book 3 of the *Nicomachean Ethics* are devoted to the distinction between ἑκούσια and ἀκούσια. It is customary to translate this pair of Greek terms by the English pair 'voluntary' and 'involuntary', and to use 'voluntarily' and 'involuntarily' for the cognates ἑκών and ἄκων. The English terms are certainly the heirs of the Greek terms, since the adjectives entered the language from the Latin *voluntarium* and *involuntarium* used in the medieval translations of Aristotle; but they are no longer the most appropriate or the most accurate translation in all contexts. This is largely because in English we dispose of other pairs of terms—such as 'intentionally' and 'unintentionally', 'willingly' and 'unwillingly'—which share with 'voluntarily' and 'involuntarily' the task of distinguishing and qualifying actions; whereas in Aristotle's Greek the single pair of expressions has to be used to make distinctions and qualifications of several different kinds. I shall continue to use the traditional translations despite their occasional unnaturalness: no other pair of terms fares sufficiently better in all contexts to justify departing from the tradition.

One of the difficulties in rendering ἀκούσιον/ἑκούσιον as 'voluntary/involuntary' meets us at the very beginning of *NE* 3.1. Voluntariness and involuntariness are naturally thought of as properties of actions and their consequences, but ἀκούσια and ἑκούσια appear to include some things which would not necessarily be regarded as actions at all. Aristotle commences by saying that virtue, and by implication the ἑκούσιον/ἀκούσιον distinction, concerns passion and action, πάθη and πράξεις. πράξεις means actions, no doubt, but what are πάθη? In the light of the previous book (cf. 1105b21ff) πάθη should be passions in the sense of emotions like anger, fear, and joy; but in the light of what follows the word may be being used in its very general sense of something that *happens* to someone: what a man suffers (in the archaic sense) in contrast to what he does. Some of the examples we are given to illustrate the ἀκούσιον/ἑκούσιον distinction are clearly things which happen to a man rather than things which he does: being blown off course by the wind, for instance, or being carried off by kidnappers. One class of ἀκούσια is defined as being the class of episodes whose origin is external and where no contribution is made by the agent *or the patient* (1110a2). Putting the doctrine of *NE* 3.1 in traditional terms, then, not only what a man does but also what he suffers may be voluntary or involuntary. What happens to a person without his doing—whether as a result of natural agents like the wind or of voluntary agents like hijackers—will be involuntary unless the person has contributed in some way to the outcome.

It is sometimes said that Aristotle's distinction between what is voluntary and what is involuntary is a distinction between cases which we hold a person responsible for something that happens and cases where we absolve from responsibility. Certainly, praise and blame are linked with voluntariness (1109b31) and in general it is a necessary condition for someone to be held responsible for an episode that he should have done it or let it happen voluntarily (cf. 1110a20); but the Aristotelian notion of voluntariness cannot simply be equated with that of moral or legal responsibility. Children and animals do things voluntarily (1111b9) but presumably are not to be held responsible; actions done through culpable ignorance of circumstances are certainly punishable (1114a9) but it is not made clear whether they are voluntary (1110b18–1111a1).

If voluntary episodes bring praise and blame, involuntary ones, Aristotle says, are attended with συγγνώμη and ἔλεος. Both words are ambiguous: the first may mean 'excuse' or 'pardon', the second may mean 'pity' or 'mercy'. The differences between the English terms in each pair are important: where there is mercy or pardon, a genuine fault has been committed but punishment is remitted; excuse, however, at least diminishes, and pity is totally divorced from, culpability. (For this reason there seems something offensive about the practice of granting a royal pardon to someone who is shown never to have committed the crime of which he has been found guilty.) It is possible that Aristotle was hampered by the ambiguity of the Greek word συγγνώμη. Here (1109a33) and elsewhere in *NE* 3 (1111a1) he says that it is involuntariness which deserves συγγνώμη. But discussing the topic of duress (1110a24) he says that if a man does something wrong out of fear of torture beyond human power to resist, then he deserves συγγνώμη: this is a context where he has made clear that he thinks actions under duress are voluntary (1110a15). One way to free his thought from inconsistency is to take him as using συγγνώμη sometimes as 'excuse' and sometimes as 'pardon', saying that we are excused for what is involuntary, and sometimes pardoned for what is voluntary.

In the *Nicomachean Ethics* Aristotle illuminates voluntariness principally by discussing different types of involuntariness. Involuntary episodes he subdivides into those involving force (βία) and those involving error (ἄγνοια). In cases of force, the episode is the result of an external agent or cause (ἀρχή): there is a chain of physical causation leading through the patient or apparent agent to some other source. Thus—to take examples provided not by Aristotle but by his commentators—if a child is picked up by his father and whirled around by main force, he is moving involuntarily; if a courtier's elbow is jerked in a press so that he strikes the monarch, the blow is an involuntary one. Not every such episode would be, for Aristotle, a case of involuntariness: he adds the further condition that the agent or patient must make no contribution. If the father is whirling the child because the child begged him to do so, or if the jostled courtier thumps the monarch harder than he is forced to, they may be said to have contributed to the outcome. Without such positive cooperation on the part of an agent it seems that something forced might fail to be involuntary in other ways: perhaps the agent fails to resist when he could; or, though he can do nothing to prevent the episode, he may be pleased when it happens. A man carried by strong winds to the port of his choice may be forced there, but not unwillingly so. In the light of what Aristotle later says about taking pleasure in actions performed in error (1110b20) he should perhaps regard such cases as not involuntary.

Aristotle goes on to consider whether cases of duress and necessity are to be considered voluntary or involuntary. If they are involuntary, clearly they will be cases of force, not of error. In English, when we speak of being forced to do something we may refer either to physical compulsion or to the fear of greater evils: not all force is main force. A man may be forced to drive his car on to the pavement to avoid running over a child; this does not mean that any physical compulsion was used on him. Both physical force and the threat of force may excuse or extenuate: but as Aristotle goes on to argue, the two cases are quite distinct. In the one case there is a manifest chain of physical causation passing through the agent; in the other the chain of physical causation comes to an end with the agent who desires to avoid the greater evil: 'The movement of the limbs that are the instruments of action has its origin in the agent himself' (1110a15). A tyrant who forces his victim to act by threatening his wife and children, though responsible for what is done, brings it about not by physical causation but by providing strong reasons for acting.

Now if a man does something base to save his wife and children from death at the tyrant's hand, is his action voluntary or involuntary? Aristotle gives no direct answer to this question but goes on to consider the case of jettisoning merchandise during a storm at sea. Gauthier and Jolif suggest that the first case presents a moral problem (should the tyrant's victim be blamed?) and that the second is meant to illuminate the problem by comparing it with a case in which praise and blame are not in question, where someone is simply disposing of his own property (1959, 177). Perhaps: but Aristotle may equally well have had in mind the legal problems raised when the master of a vessel jettisons a cargo which is not his own. The two cases are in any case distinct since the threatened evil is in one case the result of natural forces and in the other the outcome of human malevolence: in English legal terminology, the tyrant's victim is under duress, the jettisoning is a case of necessity. Aristotle offers an answer to the case of necessity and leaves us to draw our conclusions about the case of duress.

The judgment about the jettisoning is far from clear. Literally:

> In the abstract no one throws away voluntarily, but to save the life of himself and his crew any sensible man will do so. Such actions, then, are mixed, but are more like voluntary ones; for at the moment of being performed they are objects of choice. The τέλος of an action depends on the occasion: so the moment of action is when the terms 'voluntary' and 'involuntary' are to be applied. So the man acts voluntarily.

It is hard to tell in this passage when Aristotle is speaking about classes of action, and when about individual actions: the mode of expression is clumsy. A bizarre metaphysic seems implied, according to which one and the same individual action may have certain properties before being performed and others while being performed, and may have certain properties if it is performed and different properties if it is not performed. There is no such thing, we feel inclined to say, as throwing away in the abstract; any act of throwing away will occur at a certain time, in certain circumstances, and with certain aims, and it will be these factors which individuate it as the act it is (cf.1110b5). Moreover, the passage contains a number of particular ambiguities: does 'objects of choice' (αἱρεταί) mean 'chosen' or 'choiceworthy'. Is the τέλος of an action its goal or its completion?

What Aristotle wishes to express is this. If an action is to be voluntary, then there will be a description of the action which will be a description of something the agent wants to do. But actions can be variously described: the conduct of the ship's master, for instance, can be reported thus:

(1) Throwing the cargo overboard

or thus:

(2) Throwing the cargo overboard to save oneself and one's crew.

(1) as it stands is not a description of anything anyone would want to do, whereas (2) describes a course of action which would

commend itself to any man of sense. Since both descriptions are truly applicable to the master's action, it is 'mixed': it can be described either as wanted or unwanted. But when we are classifying actions as voluntary it is the more complete description that is appropriate, the description including the relevant circumstances. So, all things considered, the master's action is voluntary.

This interpretation catches the sense no matter how the ambiguities are resolved. If we take αἱρεταί to mean 'choice-worthy', then the second half of the second sentence may be understood either as

(3) The proposal 'Throw over the cargo' is attractive during the storm

or as

(4) The proposal 'Throw over the cargo during the storm' is attractive.

If we take it to mean 'chosen' we can understand it in each of the two ways in (3) and (4) with 'accepted' substituted for 'attractive'. Again, the *complete* description of the action (what gives us the τέλος in the sense of 'completion') is in this case the description (2) above which includes the purpose of the action (the τέλος in the sense of goal). We must take Aristotle to be saying not that the terms 'voluntary' and 'involuntary' are to be applied *at* the moment of action, but that they are to be applied *to* the moment of action: or rather, to the action described with the circumstances obtaining at the moment of action.

Teasing out the sense in this manner enables us to understand what Aristotle now goes on to say: 'For actions of this kind people are sometimes praised' (1110a19). What are actions 'of this kind'? A careless reading of the context would suggest actions done out of necessity or under duress. But Aristotle goes on to say 'i.e. when they put up with something disgraceful or painful for the sake of great advantage', making it clear that he has in mind not something done for fear of evil, but something borne for love of good ('for a noble object' as he said already at 1110a5). The actions are of the same kind as

actions under duress because they are cases of doing something
that considered in the abstract is unwanted and undesirable,
but which the pursuit of a desirable end makes an object of
choice.

The passage is often taken to show that Aristotle believed that
the end justifies the means. Committing adultery is shameful—
to take the second-century scholiast's illustration—but it may be
a splendid thing for a patriot to commit adultery with the
tyrant's wife in order to uncover his state secrets. Medieval
Christian admirers of Aristotle, mindful of St Paul's words 'we
must not do evils that good may come' have either condemned
Aristotle as immoral or have explained that what he had in
mind was acts which were not wicked but merely improper—
adopting a suggestion of Aspasius they took as an example the
wearing of women's clothes by a man. In fact the language
Aristotle uses here ('when they *endure* something shameful or
painful') suggests that he has in mind here not the positive performance of evil for good ends, but rather submission to suffering and disgrace (for instance, being sent to prison) for the sake
of a great and noble cause (for instance, opposition to an unjust
order in wartime). Such endurance, if it is praiseworthy, must
a fortiori be voluntary: but the question whether action under
duress is voluntary, set at 1111a7, has not yet been answered.
For all that has been said so far, it could be that Aristotle's view
was that resistance to duress is voluntary, but submission to
duress is not.

This interpretation is reinforced by the following paragraph,
which suggests that the most a man can hope for, if he performs
actions which he ought not to perform, even under the threat of
inhuman torture, is pardon or excuse, not praise. And even
συγγνώμη will not be granted to everything which is done for the
avoidance of such evil. Some things, such as matricide, are so
bad that it seems impossible to conceive a greater evil whose
avoidance will justify their performance. Alcmaeon in Euripides' lost tragedy had as good a case as one could hope for: he
claimed to be forced to kill his mother to escape his dying
father's curse. But this is not enough: 'There are some things we
cannot be forced to do; we should rather die in horrible tor-
ment' (1110a27).

When someone performs a deed less heinous than this under pressure which overstrains human nature, do we have a case of involuntariness or pardonable voluntary wrongdoing? If we recall 1109b32, and treat συγγνώμη as unambiguous, we must say such cases are involuntary: on the other hand, the arguments to prove that actions under necessity are voluntary would seem to apply also to such actions under duress. Moreover, if Alcmaeon's action is not forced it must be voluntary (for error, the other source of involuntariness, is not in question here); but if Alcmaeon acts voluntarily, then why not a lesser wrongdoer?

One may indeed wonder whether Aristotle is here settling a question of philosophy of mind or a question of morality. Surely, one might feel, he should say: either that one *cannot* be forced to do certain things, because people *will* rather die; or that one *ought not* to let oneself be forced to do certain things, because people *ought* rather to die. But what he says is that one *cannot* be forced because one *ought* to die; which appears to be the drawing of a factual conclusion from a moral premise. Is not this objectionable?

The realms of fact and value certainly cannot be neatly distinguished in the way that the objection suggests. Very often the natural description of facts involves appeal to tacit evaluations. What a person is said to have done, for instance, may well depend on what he ought to have done. This is most obvious in the case of acts of omission. Whether somebody left the door open, or let a child drown, will depend *inter alia* on whether he should have closed the door and whether what he was doing instead of rescuing the child was of comparable importance to the saving of the child's life. Aristotle is surely right that whether we accept a plea that someone was forced to act to escape a greater evil will depend on our comparative evaluation of the evils in question.

Whether an action was voluntary or not, however, does not depend on such evaluation. An action which is done in order to avoid evil is an intentional action and *a fortiori* a voluntary one: being forced, in this sense, in no way rules out being voluntary. To accept the motorist's excuse that he was forced to mount the pavement to avoid the child is not to deny that he took a decision, it is to endorse the decision that he took. If Aristotle thought that actions under duress or in necessity were not ἑκούσια then, to the extent that ἑκούσιον means 'voluntary', he was mistaken.

But did he think so? The text of *NE* 3 does not clearly say so. The verb 'to force' (ἀναγκάζειν) is not cognate with the word for 'force' (βία) which designates one category of the involuntary; in the present chapter it is only in the mouth of an objector (1110b10) that the two are linked in such a way that ἀναγκάζειν involves βία. We are told (1110a34) that praise and blame are given in the case of those who are forced or not. If this entails that people can be blamed for being forced, then in the light of 1109b31 this must mean that one can be forced and yet act voluntarily.

Aristotle draws attention to two different ways in which one may fail to behave rightly in the face of threatened evil: to make the wrong judgment in comparing what is to be done and what is to be avoided; and to make the right judgment but fail to carry it out. Here we have a distinction in wrong attitudes when faced with pain parallel to the distinction between the intemperate and incontinent *vis-à-vis* the prospect of pleasure.

The question, then, of 1110a7, whether actions done under duress are voluntary, is answered, though not quite unambiguously, in the affirmative; the question whether evildoing under duress is pardonable is answered by a distinction; and the question whether doing evil that good may come is praiseworthy is not answered or asked at all.

Prima facie there are three possible ways in which something external to an agent can make him act. One is by main force, one is by threat, and the third is by enticement or provocation. Aristotle twice considers, and twice rejects, the suggestion that crimes of lust and rage are involuntary. Commentators tell us that he has in mind the characters of Euripides who claimed to be the slaves of passion, or the Helen of Gorgias who blames her adultery on the compulsion of Aphrodite. To this suggestion Aristotle could reply that actions performed out of lust or rage cannot be involuntary since the chain of physical causation begins with the agent (as at 1110a15). He does not do this but offers a series of arguments of unequal clarity and cogency. If the satisfaction of sensual impulses was involuntary and βίαιον it would be painful, he says; but in fact it is pleasant (1110b11ff, 1111a32). If we say that actions from desire or in anger are involuntary, then the actions of children and beasts will be involuntary (1111a25ff); if we go further and say that not only is the prospect of pleasure compelling but so too is the prospect of doing something fine and noble, then no actions at all will be voluntary, because all of us do everything that we do in pursuit of either pleasure or nobility as ultimate goals (cf. *NE* 2.3, 1104b31). A resolute psychological determinist, who believed all human actions to be determined by motives, might assent to this conclusion without demur: but Aristotle goes on to talk, at 1110b13, as if he had in mind an opponent who is a determinist in respect of bad actions, and a libertarian in respect of good. 'It is absurd,' he says, 'to blame external forces and not to blame oneself for being an easy catch; to make oneself responsible for one's noble actions and to blame pleasant objects for one's base actions.'

Aristotle's target here may seem nowadays to be a straw man; but comparable partial determinisms are still with us: we are all familiar with the kind of social reformer who regards the actions of criminals as the unavoidable outcome of heredity or environment while treating the activities of judges as objects of justified moral censure, and we have all met novice revolutionaries who regard the excesses of one type of regime as indicative of the ruthless selfishness of capitalists while explaining the excesses of contrasting regimes as the inevitable outcome of a certain stage in an inexorable historical process. Aristotle is surely correct to think that the boundary between the voluntary and the involuntary cannot be drawn on the basis of a distinction between acts of which one approves and acts of which one disapproves. But the details of his argument, in *NE* 3, are intolerably obscure.[1]

1 A major difficulty is the relationship between the two treatments of the topic at 1110b3ff and 1111a24ff: commentators are no doubt right to see these two passages as doublets reflecting two different strata of composition or editing. Particular difficulties include the following: (a) How can the opponent who thinks that noble objects exercise compulsion (1110b9) be represented as holding himself responsible for his noble actions (1110b25)? Some commentators escape this difficulty by taking only the second καλά to mean noble actions, interpreting the first as beautiful bodies. But this in-

volves foisting on Aristotle the view that everything we ever do is done for the sake of pleasure or beautiful bodies (1110b11). (b) At 1111a28 Aristotle asks 'Is it meant that *no* act done through appetite or anger is voluntary, or that we do the noble actions voluntarily and the base ones involuntarily? Is not this absurd when one and the same thing is the cause?' What does Aristotle mean by 'one and the same thing': does he mean the agent, or his passion? If the agent, then he is begging the question against his opponent, who says that in crimes of passion the agent is not the cause but the victim of force. If the passion, how on his own view can a noble action be the result of passion? (cf. *NE* 2.1, 1105a28ff). (c) At 1111a30 Aristotle argues: 'It would surely be absurd to describe as involuntary things one ought to desire: but we ought to be angry at certain things, and desire certain things, e.g. health and learning.' The argument that if we can have a duty to be angry, anger must be to some extent in our power is clear, but the argument about desire (ἐπιθυμία) seems to depend on an equivocation: Aristotle's opponent is talking about desire in the narrow sense of sensual appetite, and Aristotle's reply to him depends upon taking it in the broadest sense in which even learning can be an object of desire. (d) Aristotle asks: 'What is the difference in respect of involuntariness between doing wrong after calculation and in a fit of passion? For both are to be avoided; but the irrational passions are not less human than reason is.' It seems untrue to Aristotle's general position in the *NE* to say that the irrational passions are not less human than reason; but in any case what is the relevance of this since voluntariness is something shared by brutes? Moreover, to say that both are to be avoided is not to the point; Aristotle's other arguments rest on the separability of the distinction between goodness and badness and the voluntary/involuntary distinction.

4. *Force and Involuntariness in the* Eudemian Ethics

What corresponds in the *Eudemian Ethics* to the confused Nicomachean discussion of crimes of passion is a long and carefully constructed section in chapter 8 of book II devoted to the question whether the continent and incontinent man acts voluntarily or involuntarily. This is embedded in a section which relates the question of force *vs.* voluntariness with the role played in Aristotle's general physical theory of motion and change by the concept of βία. In this most general use the word βία is better translated by 'violence' than 'force'; in Aristotle's physics a distinction is made between motions and changes which are natural and those which are violent: a distinction which has left as a trace in post-Aristotelian English the distinction between violent and natural death. Physical objects, for Aristotle, had their natural or proper places: motion towards a natural place was natural motion, and motion away from a natural place was violent motion. Thus a stone moved upward, and a fire moved downwards, not by nature but by violence (βία): stones have to be forced up, and fires forced down (1224a16–17). Aristotle offers as a definition of this kind of motion 'motion caused by an external agent against the object's internal tendency' (1224a22; cf. 1224b6). This general definition of violence (βία), he goes on to show, applies also to the force (βία) which contrasts with voluntariness in the case of living and sentient beings.

In the case of inanimate things there is a simple contrast between forced and unforced movement, because inanimate things, for Aristotle, have only a single internal tendency to motion; so too, in the case of animals who have desires but no reason, a piece of behaviour is either voluntary or compelled in an unambiguous way (the *Magna Moralia*, 1188b6, offers the example of a horse being forced to go in a direction different from that in which it wants to go). But in the case of human beings matters are more complicated once they have grown old enough to have the use of reason: for reason and desire may not agree and then we shall have two conflicting internal tendencies to take account of when assessing behaviour as voluntary or involuntary.

The possibilities of conflict are illustrated in the case of the continent and incontinent man. The incontinent man is one who reasons that he ought to act one way, but acts in another way because he yields to passion pulling in the opposite direction. The continent man, for Aristotle, is like the incontinent man in having unruly passions which tempt to act against reason: unlike the incontinent man, however, he successfully resists temptation and acts in accordance with reason's dictates. (In the really virtuous man there are no unruly desires: situations which would tempt the continent man no longer tempt him; hence he has no internal conflict but an inward calm.) Now are the actions of the continent and incontinent man voluntary? Or do they fall within the definition of force and violence ($\beta i a$) which seems to be the opposite of voluntariness (1224a13)? Aristotle proceeds to show that the case can be argued either way.

Take first the continent man. It can be argued that his action is a case of $\beta i a \iota o \nu$, because he is acting against the tendency of desire. In English as in Greek there are idioms which support this view: we speak of self-control as a matter of doing violence to oneself. The continent man full of desire, Aristotle says, has to drag himself by force away from pleasure; he acts reluctantly and painfully (1224a34). On the other hand, we can argue that the continent man acts voluntarily: for we make a contrast between force and persuasion or conviction ($\pi \epsilon \iota \theta \dot{\omega}$), and the continent man acts in accordance with his convictions and therefore not by force but voluntarily (1224a14; 1224b1). So we can argue both that continent action is voluntary and that it is a case of force.

Similarly with the incontinent. What he does is not painful but pleasant: he enjoys his pursuit of sensual delight. Since he

D

feels no distress or reluctance his action is voluntary, not enforced. On the other hand, he does not act from conviction: sensual appetite does not persuade one, but drags one by main force. So the incontinent man, like the continent man, seems both to act voluntarily and to be the victim of force.[1]

In fact, nothing gets in the way of a right understanding of voluntariness more than the idea that someone can act both voluntarily and by force (1225a35). Here we have a certain analogy to the case of violent motion in inanimate objects—we do have motion against an internal tendency. But for the definition of violence to be satisfied, rest or motion contrary to internal tendency has to be the result of an external force: but in the continent and incontinent man the dominant force is an internal tendency—will in the case of the continent man and appetite in the case of the incontinent man—so here we have neither violence nor force. Violence must originate from an external force—as when someone seizes my hand and makes me strike a third party against both my will and my appetite. We can say, if we like, that particular parts of the soul of the continent and incontinent man have force done to them; and this is what gives plausibility to saying that the continent man acts involuntarily (for his appetite suffers violence from his reason) and that the incontinent man acts involuntarily (for his reason is knocked out by his appetite). But the whole soul, the whole person, acts voluntarily (1224b22–28).

If we divide motions into violent and natural motions, the actions of the continent and incontinent are natural rather than violent: for in each case the action has its origin in a part of the soul which belongs to a human being by nature. Appetite is innate in the sense of being present and operative from birth; reason is innate in the sense that it is the outcome of normal maturation (like grey hair and old age). Though the continent and incontinent are therefore acting each against a natural principle, a different one in each case, the answer to the unqualified question 'Do they act in accordance with nature?' is 'Yes' (1224b35).

---

[1] At 1224b2 the text should read δοκοῦσιν οὗτοι μόνοι βίᾳ καὶ ἑκόντες ποιεῖν. The emendation ἑκόντες for ἄκοντες is as modest as Ross's μόνον for μόνοι and gives a better sense. It is supported by 1224b38.

The discussion of the continent and incontinent man in *EE*
ii.8 can be summarised thus briskly, because the argument is
clear and convincing and the conclusion, that actions done out of
passion are voluntary, is in accord with the position argued for
less elaborately in *NE* 3. But when we come to the second half
of *EE* ii.8 and turn to the consideration of duress the text
becomes more difficult to follow and the doctrine seems to
diverge significantly from the Nicomachean theory. Certain
types of duress, and certain types of passion, it seems, do render
action involuntary after all. But to grasp the exact force of the
Eudemian teaching here it is necessary to examine the text
closely.

At first, all seems reasonably clear (1225a2–8):

There is another way in which men are said to act under
force and coercion (βίᾳ καὶ ἀναγκασθέντες) without there being
any clash of reason with desire, when they do something they
consider painful and shameful, but are threatened with
stripes, imprisonment or death if they do not do it. Such acts
they say they did under coercion. Or is this wrong, and do
they all just what they do voluntarily? For it was in their
power not to do it, and to endure the suffering.

The second answer in this passage seems to be, more clearly and
tersely put, the one which we teased out from the Nicomachean
discussion. Here Aristotle does not seem satisfied with it, but
goes on to draw further distinctions:

One might further say that some such cases are voluntary
and others not. When it is in the agent's power whether such
a situation should obtain or not, then in every case[1] the agent
is acting voluntarily, and not under force, in doing what he
does not wish to do; when the situation is not in his control,
then he is acting under force in a manner, but not without
qualification: he does not choose what he actually does, but
he does choose the purpose for which it is done (1225a10–14).

[1] Reading μὴ ὑπάρξαι ἢ ὑπάρξαι with the MSS and rejecting Spengel's
emendation μὴ πρᾶξαι ἢ πρᾶξαι; but accepting Bonitz's alterations of δεῖ
to ἀεί.

The sense of the Greek clause translated 'when it is in the agent's power whether such a situation should obtain or not' is not clear, and some scholars have wished to emend the text to read 'whenever in these cases it is in the agent's power to perform the action or not'. But this emendation wrecks the sense of the next passage: for if it is not in the agent's power not to act, then he is acting under force not just 'in a manner' but 'without qualification'. If the *textus receptus* is translated as above we can take Aristotle to be distinguishing between cases where the existence of the duress is due to the victim's own action and cases where it is not.

The distinction is not an idle one but was very recently enforced in British courts. In the case of *Lynch v. D.P.P. for Northern Ireland*, which concerned an appellant who had been forced by I.R.A. gunmen to drive them to and from a place where they shot a policeman, the House of Lords decided that duress was a defence to a charge of murder in cases where the accused was not the actual killer or principal in the first degree. But in this and subsequent cases it has been made clear that the defence of duress is not available to an accused who, by voluntarily joining a terrorist organisation, has put himself in a position in which he may be forced to carry out the orders of that organisation under pain of being himself killed or maimed by its officers. Aristotle's choice of words is quite naturally taken as expressing agreement with the view that duress which is the result of the agent's own action does not excuse from responsibility or negative voluntariness.

Assuming that the duress is in no way the agent's fault, Aristotle goes on to say: 'He is acting under force in a manner, but not without qualification.' He seems here to be making the point that was made about necessity in *NE* 1110a9: when an agent reluctantly does x to avoid a greater evil y, x is not something that he wants, but x-rather-than-y is. The point is made rather elliptically by saying 'He chooses the purpose for which it is done': consistent with Aristotle's general view that it is means, not ends, that are chosen (1226a7) he must mean 'He chooses to do it for the purpose for which it is done'. The terminology 'without qualification' (ἁπλῶς) is used in an opposite manner in the two treatises: in the *NE* we are told that the performance of x is ἁπλῶς not voluntary (but voluntary in all the circumstances); in the *EE* we are told that it is ἁπλῶς not a matter of force (though it is enforced in a manner). The switch in the sense of ἁπλῶς is confusing: in the *NE* the term is applied to the action described in the abstract ('without qualification' in the sense that no qualifying factors are included in the description) in the present passage of the *EE* to the action described in full detail ('without qualification' in the sense that no qualifying factors remain to be specified.) But there seems, so far, to be no real difference of substance between the *NE* view and the *EE* one.[1]

Matters now become more complicated:

> Even here, cases differ. If a man were to kill in order to avoid being caught at blind-man's buff it would be ridiculous to claim that he acted under force and coercion: it has to be a greater and more painful evil that he will suffer if he does not do the deed. (1225a19–23)

Is this condition meant to be a necessary condition for acting involuntarily, or for acting under force *in a manner*? What has been said so far, and the analogy with the *NE*, would lead us to suggest that someone who acts to avoid a greater evil still acts voluntarily, and is only *in a manner* forced. But what comes next gives us pause:

> Thus he will act under coercion—and not by force or in an unnatural way—when he does something evil for the sake of good, or in order to escape from a greater evil, and involuntarily, these matters not being in his power.

This passage is undoubtedly most naturally interpreted as saying, in contradiction to the *NE* position, that actions done to

---

[1] It is perhaps possible to translate the crucial passage thus: 'He is acting under force in a manner—not without qualification, which would mean that he does not choose what he actually does, but with respect to the purpose of his choice.' This would not lessen the difficulty about ἁπλῶς, but it would relieve the problem about the choice of ends; but it presupposes a Greek construction too telegrammatic perhaps even for Aristotle.

avoid a greater evil are voluntary. But there are several
difficulties in interpreting the Greek text. All MSS read 'under
coercion and not by force' (ἀναγκαζόμενος καὶ μὴ βίᾳ); since
elsewhere in the *EE* and *NE* coercion and force seem to be
treated more or less as equivalent, and since if the conduct is
not enforced it is hard to see why Aristotle should go on to say
that it is involuntary, several editors and commentators suggest
deleting the 'not' or replacing it by 'or' (ἢ for μή), and understand the text as meaning that action under duress is involuntary, coerced, enforced, and unnatural.

The emendation is not necessarily unavoidable. 'Not by force
or in an unnatural way' can be read, as in the translation suggested above, as a parenthesis (μή βίᾳ ... ἢ οὐ φύσει). This
reading is confirmed by the fact that the *Magna Moralia*, in the
corresponding passage (1.15, 1188b20ff) counts action to avoid
greater evils (the example given is cutting short one's stay in
order to avoid one's crops being ruined) as an instance of ἀνάγκη
but not of βία. If supporters of the emendation point a few lines
further down to 1224b23 to where Aristotle says that someone
who acts to escape pain would seem to act involuntarily and
under force, it can be replied that he merely says that such a person *would seem* (δόξειε) so to act, using an expression he frequently
employs to record the views of others without committing himself to them.

The more important point, however, is whether Aristotle is
saying that action under duress is involuntary, whether or not
it is enforced. This is what he is saying if the 'and involuntarily'
(καὶ ἄκων γε) in the quoted passage is taken with the verb of the
main clause 'will act under coercion', rather than with the verb
of the 'when'-clause 'does something evil'. In favour of taking it
with the main verb it may be said that there would be something circular in including involuntariness among the conditions to be satisfied for an action to count as coerced; in
favour of taking it with the nearby verb it may be said that all
the distinctions Aristotle has so far drawn are pointless if he is
going to count all action for the sake of good or avoidance of
evil as being involuntary. Moreover, such action is strictly
speaking the result of choice (1225a12); *a fortiori*, then, it is
voluntary.

If we take 'involuntarily' with the verb of the subordinate clause, we can avoid circularity if we take Aristotle to be referring to the involuntariness of the circumstances in which the agent is acting—the necessity to do evil to achieve the good, or avoid the greater evil—so that 'these matters' which are not in the agent's power are the overall situation, referred to at 1225a10–11, which presents him with the painful choice. Taken thus, Aristotle is saying that acts under duress are coerced (the agent acts ἀναγκαζόμενος) provided that the duress itself is involuntary; but he has not committed himself to the view that they are involuntary except in the sense of being 'enforced in a manner'. This would make the *EE* doctrine the same as that of the *NE* except for the added proviso about the involuntariness of the duress.

Aristotle now returns to the question whether passion renders action involuntary:

> Hence many regard love and some kinds of anger and physical conditions as involuntary, because they are strong and beyond nature: we extend indulgence, because they are things capable of doing violence to nature.

The force of the 'hence' is not clear: it must be something like 'It is for a similar reason that . . .' Note that it is not the actions done out of love or rage that are being considered as involuntary, but these states themselves: which confirms the view that in the immediately preceding passage it was the voluntariness of the overall situation that was in question. A preternaturally strong passion puts its victim in the same helpless position as a tyrant's prisoner.

Aristotle does not say explicitly here whether he agrees with those who regard love as involuntary: from his final summing up of the question it appears that he does.[1] What he is talking about are not the normal passions of normal human beings:

---

[1] The word translated 'indulgence' above is the ambiguous συγγνώμη, meaning pardon or excuse, which caused difficulty in the understanding of the corresponding passage in the *NE* discussed above. The *EE* does not commit itself to the view that συγγνώμη entails involuntariness; but at 1228a10 it says that involuntary evils are not blamed.

those have already been discussed in the lengthy treatment of incontinence, and it has been made clear that they do not render action involuntary. What he has in mind is a pathologically strong ἔρως, a phenomenon as out of the ordinary as the inspired utterances of a prophetess in a trance:

> What depends on him—and it all comes back to this—is what his nature is able to bear; what is not, and what is not the result of his own natural desire and reasoning, does not depend on him. For this reason those who are rapt and who prophesy, though what they produce is a product of thought, we do not say that it depends on them to say what they say or to do what they do. So too with the results of appetite. So that some thoughts and passions do not depend on us, and neither do the acts which result from such thoughts and reasonings. (1224a25–33)

The 'results of appetite' in this passage, if it is not to be a flat contradiction of the treatment of incontinence, must be the results of preternaturally strong appetite, appetite which contrasts with 'his own natural desire'.

The most puzzling question raised by the passage is this: in what way is the sudden introduction of preternaturally strong passion and preternaturally prophetic utterance intended to be relevant to the topic of duress and necessity and doing evil that good may come? The connection seems to be this. There are some threats which are so terrible that only a person of supernatural bravery could resist them: pains so strong that the natural fears of a normal person will lead him to do anything to avoid them.[1] In these cases, as in the case of someone out of their mind with love, we are to 'extend indulgence, because they are things capable of doing violence to nature'.

Each of the three parts into which Plato divided the soul—reason, temper, and appetite—can operate in a natural or

---

[1] This is why at 1225a22 Aristotle remarks that acting to avoid strong pain would appear to be more involuntary than acting to avoid slight pain, and acting to avoid pain more so than acting to gain pleasure. (Here, unlike line 17 above, the deletion of the μή in the MSS reading ἵνα μὴ χαίρῃ seems imperative.)

preternatural manner. The preternatural operation of reason is prophecy; the preternatural operation of appetite is exhibited in the consuming passion of a Medea; the preternatural operation of temper (θυμός) may be shown either in a crime committed in overmastering rage or in resistance to an overwhelming pressure. It is when reason, temper, and appetite are operating normally that we have voluntary behaviour: virtuous, vicious, continent or incontinent as the case may be. In the case of the preternatural operation of temper and passion we are reminded of the persons of heroic virtue and brutish vice described at the beginning of the third of the books common to the *EE* and *NE* (1145a15ff).

If we interpret the Eudemian text in this way, we obtain the following classification of actions done under duress with respect to voluntariness (ἑκούσιον), force (βία) and coercion (ἀνάγκη):

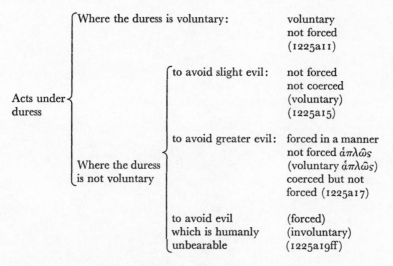

Acts under duress	Where the duress is voluntary:		voluntary not forced (1225a11)
	Where the duress is not voluntary	to avoid slight evil:	not forced not coerced (voluntary) (1225a15)
		to avoid greater evil:	forced in a manner not forced ἁπλῶς (voluntary ἁπλῶς) coerced but not forced (1225a17)
		to avoid evil which is humanly unbearable	(forced) (involuntary) (1225a19ff)

So interpreted, the Eudemian doctrine on duress is fairly close to the Nicomachean one. Both adopt the same broad pattern of distinctions, but only the Eudemian draws the distinction between duress which is itself voluntary and duress which is itself involuntary, and only the Nicomachean distinguishes, in cases where the threatened evil is humanly unbearable, be-

Aristotle's Theory of the Will

tween acts so heinous as to be inexcusable and those lesser crimes which deserve συγγνώμη if committed under duress. As already observed, the Eudemian terminology and the Nicomachean terminology differ: only the *EE* explicitly distinguishes between force and coercion, and the two treatises employ the distinction between ἁπλῶς and πως in opposite senses.

On the topic of enticement and provocation the *EE* agrees with the *NE* that the lusts and rages of a normal human being do not negative voluntariness or excuse from responsibility. But unlike the *NE* the *EE* makes room for extreme pathological passions as an excusing factor. Concerning crimes of passion no less than crimes under duress the *EE* is more lenient than the *NE*: Medea and Simon Peter would be more gently treated in a Eudemian court than in a Nicomachean one.

5. Voluntariness, Knowledge and Error in the Ethics

The second class of involuntary acts considered in *NE* 3 consists of things happening δι' ἄγνοιαν. This phrase is most naturally translated as 'through ignorance'; but both from the examples given and from Aristotle's usage elsewhere it is clear that ἄγνοια includes not just lack of knowledge, but also positively mistaken belief.[1] 'Error' seems the best translation to capture this breadth of meaning. Aristotle distinguishes between doing something *in* error (ἀγνοῶν) and doing it *through* error or *because of* error (δι' ἄγνοιαν) (110b24ff). Men who are drunk or angry or wicked may act *in* error without acting *through* error. The distinction seems to be between cases in which the agent is not responsible for the error and cases in which the error depends in some way on himself. A drunk may act in a certain way as a result of a mistake he makes (mistaking a policeman, perhaps, for a barmaid), but his mistake is itself the result of his drinking, so that Aristotle will not say that his action was *because of* his mistake: we must mention the less immediate cause and say that it was because of his drunkeness: he acts *in* error but not *through* error. So too with an angry man: Aristotle must be thinking of someone in a blind rage who does not stop to think what he is doing. The wicked man too is in error: he is mistaken about what he should do and what he should avoid. But he does not act involuntarily, or through error:

> An act can hardly be called involuntary because the agent is in error about what is expedient: it is not error in one's pur-

---

[1] At 1110b29 Aristotle refers to one kind of ἄγνοια as ἁμαρτία; and see *Topics*, 148a8.

posive choice that makes one's action involuntary—it makes it wicked—nor error about the universal—which invites blame—but error about particulars, the circumstances of the action and the objects it concerns.

It is clear that the type of error mentioned here as non-excusing is being contrasted with simple errors of fact, such as a mistake about the nature of a dose that one is giving to a patient. But it is not clear why Aristotle should treat 'error about what is expedient' 'error about the universal' 'error in one's purposive choice' as equivalent expressions—if indeed he does so. A purposive choice, we are shortly to be told (1114a4) is a decision after deliberation: but does not the sort of reasoning leading to a decision include both universal and particular premises? Consider the practical reasoning of Don Giovanni presented in Aristotelian form:

(A) It is a splendid thing to seduce other men's wives
(B) Here is another man's wife
(C) So I'll seduce her.

(A) seems a clear enough example of something that Aristotle would regard as both universal error (ἡ καθόλου ἄγνοια) and as error about what is expedient (ἄγνοια of τὰ συμφέροντα, the things that conduce to a good life). But the 'purposive choice' seems in the light of the definition of 1114a4 to be (C), not (A); and since (C) is derived from both (A) and (B) why should an erroneous judgment like (A) count as 'error in one's purposive choice' (ἐν τῇ προαιρέσει ἄγνοια) rather than an erroneous judgment of fact to the effect of (B)—the judgment, for instance, made by the unfortunate Count in the final act of *The Marriage of Figaro*?

That problem must wait until we have considered Aristotle's full account of the nature of purposive choice. But, assuming that, for whatever reason, Aristotle is using the expression 'error in one's purpose' to refer to erroneous judgments such as (A), there still seems a difficulty in saying *tout court* that people get blamed on account of error about general moral principles. May there not be some moral issues on which men of equal good will equally well qualified to judge may reach opposite conclusions of principle? And even in cases where there can be no question that particular moral principles are evil, whether a man can be blamed for holding them surely depends in part on what chances he had of acquiring better ones. The sweeping nature of Aristotle's statement here could only really be justified by belief in a universal natural law which was within the grasp of all men.

If Aristotle seems too severe on the topic of universal error, he seems too easygoing on the topic of particular error. A mistake about any particular circumstance, he says, makes an action involuntary. He gives several examples of the kind of thing he has in mind: a man giving away a secret which he did not know was meant to be secret; an instructor who lets off a catapult while demonstrating its use to a learner; a person killing a son by mistake for an enemy, as Merope nearly did in Euripides' lost *Cresphontes*; a fencer using an unprotected foil under the mistaken impression that it had the button on; a boxer injuring his sparring partner by a blow that was meant as a light touch; and so forth. The list makes clear how broad is Aristotle's category of error. The examples are meant to illustrate the different features of an action about which one can be in error: if you are giving away a secret or letting off a catapult, you may not know *what* you are doing ($\tau\acute{\iota}$); Merope did not know *whom* she was proposing to kill ($\pi\epsilon\rho\grave{\iota}$ $\tau\acute{\iota}$ or $\dot{\epsilon}\nu$ $\tau\acute{\iota}\nu\iota$); the mistake about the foil is a mistake about *what* you are doing something *with*, what you are using ($\tau\acute{\iota}\nu\iota$); a doctor prescribing a wrong drug may be mistaken about its *effects* (confusingly called here by Aristotle its $o\hat{\upsilon}$ $\dot{\epsilon}\nu\epsilon\kappa\alpha$ or purpose); the boxer does not know *how hard* he is hitting his partner ($\pi\hat{\omega}s$). But though in each case there is some feature of what he is doing that the agent does not know, not all of the cases are ones where the evil effect could be said to be the result of mistake or ignorance. The catapult goes off by accident, not as a result of error about any item of fact; the boxer lacks the intention to wound, rather than any piece of information. Moreover, many cases which would fall within Aristotle's category of error would be cases of negligence or carelessness: they are all cases of unintentional action, but not all of them are cases where the agent could hope to escape blame. A doctor prescribing a wrong potion, an incompetent artillery instructor unintentionally discharging missiles: such people are surely guilty of professional negligence and deserve censure. Actions which are involuntary through error are not, *eo ipso*, excusable:

> As error is possible with regard to any of these features, a man who acts in error with respect to any of them is considered as acting involuntarily. (1111a16–18)

When Aristotle says, in addition, that 'in these cases there is excuse and pity' we must take him as meaning 'there is *room for* excuse and pity' if his teaching is not to be impossibly over-lenient.

NE 3.1, then, leaves the impression that Aristotle is too strict concerning moral error, and too lenient about errors of fact. This impression is in part corrected when in the fifth chapter of the same book he returns to the topic. The discussion in this chapter is governed by the desire to refute the Socratic view that nobody is voluntarily wicked. Criticising this position, Aristotle appeals to penal practice. People are punished for error itself, if they are responsible for the error: thus drunkards get double penalties, because it was open to them not to get drunk, and the drunkenness was the cause of the error (1114b 30ff). He goes on:

> Moreover, people punish those who are ignorant of anything in the laws that they ought to have known and might easily have known; and so too in other cases where error seems to be due to negligence: it was in the offender's power not to err, we think, since he had the power to take care. (1114b34ff)

Is the distinction here made between things in the laws and other matters the same as the distinction earlier drawn between error about the universal and error about the particular? If so, Aristotle is now qualifying his earlier position: not all universal error is blameworthy, but only ignorance of what one should and could easily have known; not all particular error is excused, but only error which is not due to negligence. But

perhaps there is no good reason for equating the ignorance of
what is expedient in 1110b31 with the error about legal matters
of 1113b34. Perhaps ignorance of the law is just a particular
case of errors about particular circumstances, in which case it
will fall under the general principles of chapter 1; or perhaps it
is a special instance of moral error, in which case the other
matters of 1114a1 may be other moral considerations. It is not
easy to decide between these interpretations.

In *NE* 3.1 Aristotle makes a slightly puzzling connection
between involuntariness and repentance or remorse. He says
that if a man acts through error, and when he discovers his
error regrets what he has done, then he acted involuntarily;
but if he does not feel any compunction when he discovers what
he did through error, his action is not involuntary but merely
non-voluntary (he acted οὐχ ἑκών, not ἄκων) (1110b18–24).

In English as in Greek 'voluntary' and 'involuntary' are
contraries and there are many things we do which we do neither
voluntarily nor involuntarily. But it seems clear that a person's
subsequent state of mind can have very little to do with whether
a particular action is voluntary, involuntary, or neither.

Probably Aristotle has in mind cases such as Hamlet's
murder of Polonius. When Polonius hid behind the arras,
Hamlet stabbed him, believing him to be Claudius. Discovering his error, he says, unabashed:

> Thou wretched, rash, intruding fool, farewell!
> I took thee for thy better, take thy fortune.

and he shows no sign of remorse as he 'lugs the guts into the
neighbour room'. Like Aristotle, we would be inclined to say
that Hamlet did not kill Polonius voluntarily, since he did not
know he was doing so (not that that will help him much on a
murder charge, since he was killing a man voluntarily); but
whether we say he killed him involuntarily or not will not
depend on our knowledge of his subsequent callous attitude.
Probably Aristotle is here influenced by the use of ἄκων to
mean 'unwillingly' 'reluctantly': Hamlet certainly did not kill
Polonius unwillingly, or reluctantly.

The Eudemian treatment of error and involuntariness does

not make a similar link with repentance and remorse. Indeed, having identified voluntariness with a certain cognitive state (defining ἑκούσιον as τὸ κατὰ τὴν διάνοιαν, 1225b1), Aristotle deals very briefly and pregnantly with the topic of error in *EE* II.9:

> The voluntary, then, seems to be opposite to the involuntary, and acting with knowledge of the person, the instrument, and the effect—for sometimes one knows that it is one's father but not that the effect will be lethal rather than salutary, as in the case of Pelias' daughters; or knows the instrument, knowing one is giving a potion, but believing it to be a wine or a philtre, when it is really hemlock—seems to be opposite to acting in error about the person, instrument and thing, and through error not merely *per accidens*. What is done through error, whether of things, instrument, or person, is involuntary; the opposite therefore is voluntary. (1225b1–8)[1]

This excessively compressed passage is very much more intelligible to someone who reads it in the light of *NE* 3.1, or *AE* A.8 than it would be to someone who had to use it as his only evidence for Aristotle's views on involuntariness and error. The daughters of Pelias, deceived by Medea, tried to renew the youth of their father by boiling him up with herbs. They knew the person they were acting on, and in a sense they knew the instrument (though Medea had deceived them about the nature of the herbs), but they did not know the effect of their action. (Here as in *NE* 3 Aristotle confusingly uses οὗ ἕνεκα not for their purpose, which was good, but for the actual effect, which was disastrous.)

The list of relevant circumstances is shorter and less com-

[1] There are a number of problems with the Greek text of this passage. Literally Aristotle draws a contrast between a person who knows *either* the person *or* the instrument *or* the effect, and a person who is in error about the person, *and* the instrument *and* the thing. As he can hardly mean that error about *every* circumstance is necessary for involuntariness, and knowledge of *any* circumstance suffices for voluntariness, translators render the passage as if the ἤ's were καί's and *vice versa*. At 1225b4 the principal MSS read ἤτοι ὣς ὅτι μέν; the most convincing emendation is Bywater's ἢ τὸ ᾧ ὅτι μέν, which is translated in the text. I follow the Bonitz-Susemihl punctuation.

plete than that in the *NE*: of the seven circumstances listed in the Nicomachean passage only three or four appear here (three if the ὅ of lines 6 and 7 refers to the same circumstances as the οὗ ἕνεκα of line 2, otherwise four). The ὅν, or person acted on corresponds to the περὶ τί or ἐν τίνι of *NE* 1111a4; the ᾧ, or means corresponds to the instrument of *NE* 1111a15; the ὅ or 'what' probably means the thing done, the action, the τί or ὅ πράττει of *NE* 1111a4,a8; the οὗ ἕνεκα, as already remarked, appears in both *Ethics* in the sense of 'effect'. Many cases of error in action can be described either as mistakes about what one is doing or mistakes about the effect of what one is doing: the daughters of Pelias could be said to be in error about the effect of their action (they knew they were boiling him, but thought it would make him better, not kill him) or about the action itself (they thought they were rejuvenating him and in fact they were killing him). That is no doubt why Aristotle uses the triad person-means-effect and the triad person-means-deed as if they were equivalent to each other.

The description of the involuntary agent as 'acting in error about the person, means, and thing done', and 'through error not merely *per accidens*' needs further examination. One can take 'not merely *per accidens*' to be a reinforcement of 'through error', making the same contract as the Nicomachean passage makes between action *through* error and action *in* error (the latter being *per accidens*). This is how the passage is understood by Solomon, in whose translation involuntary action is described as 'action in ignorance of the person, instrument or thing, if, that is, the action is essentially the effect of ignorance'. The Nicomachean distinction between acting in error and acting through error is not foreign to the Eudemian passage, which seems to allude to it a few lines later (1225b10); but it seems that Aristotle here has a different contrast in mind. The case of the love-philtre illustrates not simply the fact that one can be in error about the means one is using, but that one can combine being in error about the morally and legally relevant features of what one is using with a certain amount of knowledge of its nature. We might say the persons sending the

---

[1] At 1135b14-16 the ὅ and the οὗ ἕνεκα are distinguished, the ὅ being in the example 'throwing (a missile)' the οὗ ἕνεκα being 'to wound'.

E

philtre knew *per accidens* what it was (a potion) but did not
know the crucial fact that it was hemlock. In *AE* A.8 (1135a25)
the terminology of *per accidens* is used to make exactly the same
point in connection with a different example.

Aristotle now gives his final summary definition of voluntariness:

> Whenever a man does something which is in his power not to
> do, and does it not in error and of his own volition, he must
> needs do voluntarily: this is what voluntariness is. What he
> does in error and through error, is involuntary. (1225b8–10)

The brief phrases of the definition take up the points which we
have seen developed at length. The restriction of the voluntary
to things which it is in a man's power not to do (the celebrated
'liberty of indifference') summarises the discussion of the way a
human being is a principle of action and rules out cases of
force. The exclusion of error resumes the immediately preceding
discussion: the proviso 'of his own volition' rules out the cases
in which coercion or passion excuses.[1]

Aristotle finally adds to his definition a distinction between
the possession and exercise of knowledge: someone may know
a piece of information relevant to his action, and yet not make
use of it in action. Can he be said to be acting in error? Yes,
says Aristotle, but only if his failure to make use of the knowledge is not due to negligence. He does not illustrate the type
of thing he has in mind: but in *AE* C the distinction between
the exercise and use of knowledge, which goes back to Plato's
Theaetetus, is exploited at considerable length when the theory of
the practical syllogism is applied to the discussion of incontinence.

As in the *Nicomachean Ethics*, so in the *Eudemian*, Aristotle
adds as an afterthought that the failure to possess a piece of
relevant information does not excuse when it was due to negligence, if it is something that the agent should and could easily
have known (1225b15). He does not in the *Eudemian Ethics*

---

[1] The expression δι' αὑτόν recalls *Rhet.* 1.10, 1368b32ff where a similar
expression is used to indicate actions done from desire or habit and to rule
out ἀνάγκη.

distinguish here between moral error and error of fact: but he goes on to add that the error may not excuse if it is due to pleasure or pain. Here again we have a cryptic remark which becomes intelligible if linked with the discussion of incontinence in *AE* c. One kind of incontinent man, we are told, does not complete his deliberation, but rushes to enjoyment (1150b20; cf. 1149a35): such a man, attracted by the prospect of seducing a woman, may not stop to inquire whether she is married, and thus unaware seduce his neighbour's wife: this would be 'error due to pleasure'. Failure to locate the enemy in battle, through unwillingness to make a reconnaissance from an exposed position, might be a case of 'error due to pain'.

Chapter 8 of *AE* A relates the topic of voluntariness and involuntariness to that of just and unjust action. It has often been remarked that the account of voluntariness which introduces the discussion is very close to that of the *Eudemian Ethics*. We read:

> By the voluntary I mean, as has been said before, what a man does of the things that are in his power, knowingly and not in error about the person, the means, or the effect (e.g. whom he is hitting, and what with, and to what effect), and in each respect not *per accidens* (nor under force, as in the case where someone takes his hand and makes him hit a third party— in such a case he does not act voluntarily, because it was not in his power); for it is possible for the person struck to be one's father and for one to know that it is a man, or one of the bystanders, and yet not to know that it is one's father; a similar distinction can be made with respect to the end, and with regard to the action as a whole. (1135a23–31)[1]

The triad of circumstances (person, means and effect), the introduction of the qualification about *per accidens* knowledge, the example given to illustrate the use of force: all these echo not the Nicomachean but the Eudemian treatment of volun-

---

[1] The punctuation of this passage in Bywater is faulty (there should be a bracket before μηδὲ βίᾳ, as in the translation above, and not after); this misled translators such as Ross and Ostwald to take ἕκαστον in line 26 to refer to actions and not to circumstances.

tariness (1225b2ff, 1225b6, 1224b13). The Eudemian definition of voluntariness rules out force by saying that the actions
in question must be in the agent's power *not to do:* here force
has to be explicitly ruled out, since the initial clause of the
definition spoke more vaguely just of 'things in his power'. The
Eudemian definition adds the qualification that the action
must be 'of his own volition' to rule out coercion: here this
qualification is not included in the definition since the topic is
about to be singled out for discussion. Like the Eudemian
chapter, the present passage states that natural processes which
are not the result of desire are neither voluntary nor involuntary (1224a18); this is so even in the case of conscious processes
in human beings: 'There are many natural processes that we
perform or undergo in full knowledge, none of which is either
voluntary or involuntary, for example, growing old or dying'
(1135a34ff)—these last being natural in the sense explained in
the *EE* at 1224b16.

Concerning duress, the chapter again appears closer to the
Eudemian than to the Nicomachean treatment. Actions can
be described as just or unjust, Aristotle says, in a *per accidens* or
incidental sense:

A man might return a deposit involuntarily and through
fear, so that we cannot say that he does what is just or acts
justly, except incidentally. Similarly, we can say that a man
acts unjustly and does what is unjust only incidentally when
he fails to return a deposit under compulsion and involuntarily. (1135b2–8, trans. Ostwald)

In the *NE*, as we have seen, actions done through fear are described as voluntary (1110a14); in the *EE* at least some actions
done through fear are involuntary (see above p. 42f). I suggested earlier that the *NE* and *EE* are reconcilable if we suppose
that the class of actions regarded as forced by the *EE* is the
same as those where human nature is overborne, as described
by *NE* 1110a23: failure to return a deposit presumably not
being so heinous as to fall under the exceptions to this exemption mentioned at *NE* 1110a28. In the present passage we are
not told how severe the threat is under which the agent acts. If

the debtor is paying up merely for fear of the normal legal processes, then there does seem to be a conflict between this text and the *NE* passage and, on our interpretation at least, the *EE* passage.

Aristotle goes on to make the distinction, common ground in all his ethical writings, between those voluntary acts which are, and those which are not, the result of purposive choice and deliberation (cf. *NE* 3.1, 1112a14–17; *EE* II.10, 1226b30–36). His interest in recalling this distinction is to connect it with the legal theme of premeditation: as indeed was promised in the passage in the *EE* where we were told:

> The legislative distinction between voluntary, involuntary and premeditated occurrences is a good one: it may not be totally precise, but at least it approximates to the truth. But we shall speak about these matters in our discussion of justice. (1226b36–27a2)

In the present passage Aristotle adds the precision which he found lacking in the broad legal categorisation by making two further subdivisions in the category of the voluntary and two further subdivisions in the category of the involuntary. Leaving aside the topic of force and coercion, which is not in question in the present passage, he distinguishes two classes of actions involuntary through error, one class being excusable and the other not (1135b11–19, 1136a6–9), and two classes of voluntary but unpremeditated actions, those done through culpable error (1135b17–19), and those done knowingly under the influence of normal passion (1135b20–22).

Injuries are cases of mistake or accident (ἁμάρτημα: no single English word quite corresponds) in the broad sense whenever an agent is in error about what he is doing, or to whom, or with what, or to what effect. But we must distinguish between cases where the injury could not reasonably have been foreseen, and where it could. If it could not have been foreseen then the accident is a case of misadventure (ἀτύχημα), and no blame attached to the agent; if it could have been foreseen then it is a case of ἁμάρτημα in the strict sense, culpable error: is it misadventure when the cause of the error is external to the agent, culpable mistake when the cause is internal.[1] The *Magna Moralia* at the corresponding points gives drunkenness as an example of an internal cause of error:

> Take for instance people who are drunk. Those who are drunk and have done something bad commit injustice. For they are themselves the causes of their ignorance. For they need not have drunk so much as not to know that they were beating their father. (1195a32ff, trans. Stock)

This accords with the *Nicomachean Ethics* in treating drunkenness as a source of non-excusing error. But the *NE* gives as another example of the same the case of a man in a rage (1110b26): the drunken and the raging man are examples of action in error but not through error. Here in the *AE*, by contrast, Aristotle goes on to list injuries committed through anger as instances of things done knowingly, though without premeditation (1135b 21). Such acts are fully, not incidentally, unjust: ἀδικήματα. It may be that Aristotle has two different cases in mind. In the *NE* he may be thinking of someone who is in such a rage that he strikes out without troubling to find out whom he is attacking and thus unknowingly assaults, say, a policeman, or his own father. In the present passage he may be thinking of someone who is so angry that he knows what he is doing but does not care: a person in a fury, say, choosing the most valuable vase in the room to pick up and hurl to the floor. Or it may be that between writing the two passages he had changed his mind about the most appropriate classification for crimes of this kind. On either account they turn out voluntary and punishable, but by different means.

Though blameworthy, acts under provocation must be distinguished from premeditated injuries:

> Acts proceeding from anger are rightly judged not to be done of malice aforethought; for it is not the man who acts in anger but he who enraged him that starts the mischief. Again, the matter in dispute is not whether the thing happened or

---

[1] I accept Jackson's emendation ἀγνοίας for αἰτίας in the sentence ἁμαρτάνει μὲν γὰρ ὅταν ἡ ἀρχὴ ἐν αὐτῷ ᾖ τῆς αἰτίας, ἀτυχεῖ δ' ὅταν ἔξωθεν.

not, but its justice; for it is apparent injustice that occasions
rage. For they do not dispute about the occurrence of the
act . . . but agreeing about the fact they dispute on which side
justice lies (whereas a man who has deliberately injured
another cannot help knowing that he has done so), so that
the one thinks he is being treated unjustly and the other disagrees. (1135b26–35, trans. Ross)[1]

Carelessly read, this passage raises difficulty: it seems to be saying that injuries inflicted under provocation are a case of error
(ἄγνοια), and thus it seems to be contradicting what immediately
precedes. But the possibility of error which is considered here is
not mistake about the nature of the injury that the provoked
agent is doing to the provoker: it is error about the provoking
injury, and about the extent to which it justifies retaliation: the
error of taking an 'apparent injustice' for a real one. Jackson
puts it well:

> For example, A, wrongly thinking himself to have been
> injured by B, strikes him in the heat of passion. Here A is
> εἰδώς in respect of his own act, but ἀγνοῶν in respect of the
> supposed injury. Hence his act is not held by the law to be
> ἐκ προνοίας. (1897, 113)[2]

There is no dispute whether A struck B: but A claims he did so
justly, because of B's previous injurious behaviour, while B
claims that A acts unjustly because no provocation is given. If
A is right, say if B has been caught *flagrante delicto* with his wife,
then there is no ἀδίκημα at all; but if B is right, then A has done
an unjust act (a) through passion (b) in knowledge of the nature

---

[1] Compare *EE* II.3, 1221b22ff: men dispute the description of their
actions as 'adultery' or 'assault': 'They say they had intercourse but did not
commit adultery (for they acted in error, or under coercion), or that they
gave a blow but did not commit assault; and so they defend themselves
against all other similar charges.'

[2] Referring to Plato, *Laws* IX. 867A, Jackson thinks that ὁ ἐπιβουλεύσας
who is contrasted with the man who acts in anger is a man who broods over
an injury and takes revenge after an interval: he has time to detect his mistake and thus has no excuse. But the contrast may well be with any form of
unprovoked malicious plotting.

and circumstances of his own act (c) in error about the nature of B's act and therefore of the justification of his own. Where the provocation was genuine, it is B who 'started the mischief' and A's action is like a case of βία where the ἀρχή or initiating cause is external; where it is only apparent, A's action is a case of ἀδίκημα through normal passion.

Having said that deliberate unjust action makes not only the action but the man unjust, Aristotle concludes the chapter thus:

> Of involuntary actions some are excusable, others not. The things which men do wrong not only in error but through error are excusable; those which they do not through error but in error due to some passion which is neither natural nor typical of human beings are not excusable. (1136a5–9)

The distinction between acting in error and through error recalls and accords with both the *NE* (1110b25) and the *EE* (1225b10). But the statement that there are some inexcusable involuntary actions clashes with *NE* 1109b32. The statement that errors due to non-natural, non-human passions do not excuse contrasts with the statement in *EE* II.8, that we feel indulgence towards passions which are strong enough to violence to nature. If the *AE* and the *EE* belong together, what is the point of first exempting actions of preternatural passion from censure as being cases of βία, and then refusing to exempt them as being cases of ἄγνοια? No ἄγνοια is present in the cases mentioned in the *EE*: but one would have expected the addition of a second head of excuse to reinforce rather than reduce the case of exemption. Perhaps the only way to reconcile the two passages is to take them as referring to two different kinds of non-natural passion: the ὑπὲρ τὴν φύσιν passions of the *EE* are passions for normal objects but of extreme force; the πάθος μήτε φυσικὸν μήτε ἀνθρώπινον of *AE* A is a perverted passion of the kind described in *AE* c.5, unnatural cruelty or lust amounting to brutishness (1184b15ff).

When we are told that crimes committed in error due to non-human passions are not excusable, does that mean that crimes committed in error due to normal passion are excusable? No: it is simply that they do not belong to the category of inexcusable *involuntary* actions: they have already been implicitly classified as voluntary at 1135b20. Many see in this classification a contradiction with the teaching of *AE* c on incontinence: is not the incontinent man, the man who gives in to normal human passion, there described as acting in a state of ἄγνοια (1147b6), whether or not he acts δι' ἄγνοιαν (1145b29)? The treatment of incontinence in *AE* c raises many difficulties; but I have argued elsewhere that in one or two passages (1147a24–1147b3, 1150b20) Aristotle recognises the possibility of incontinent action in full awareness of what one is doing, alongside the kind of incontinence which is a case of action in error (error due to pleasure) but not through error, a case parallel to that of the drunkard (1147a17). *AE* c, if I am right, allows both for actions done in error through ordinary passion, and acts done without error through ordinary passion: they form the two categories of incontinence, namely impulsive incontinence (προπέτεια) and weak-willed incontinence (ἀσθένεια), described at 1820b19ff. Both kinds of incontinence are voluntary, and both are blameworthy, as in the *EE* at 1125b15f.

The category of excusable involuntary actions coincides with that of misadventure or ἀτύχημα: the category of inexcusable involuntary actions cannot be a kind of ἀδίκημα since it is involuntary; it adds a new class of punishable injuries to those already mentioned, which corresponds in some respects to the criminally insane of more recent jurisdictions—to be exempted from responsibility but subjected to severer incarceration than the responsible criminal.

We may thus conclude our comparison of the treatments of voluntariness and involuntariness in the *NE*, *EE* and *AE*. The results of our inquiry can conveniently be presented in schematic form in the three tables which follow, each of which represents the characteristic contribution of one of the three treatments.

VOLUNTARINESS AND NON-VOLUNTARINESS IN THE *EE*

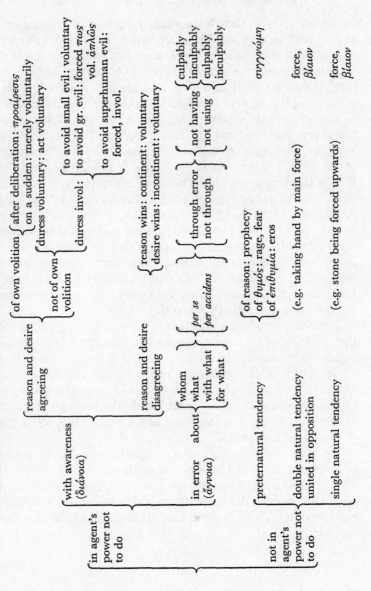

CATEGORIES OF HUMAN ACTION IN THE *NE*

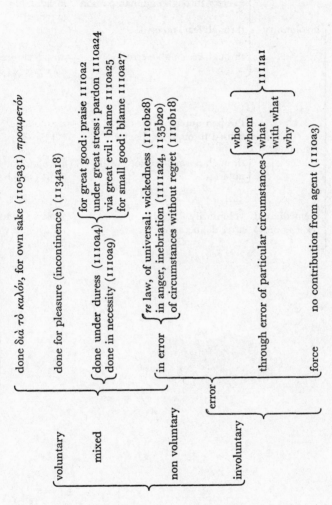

done διὰ τὸ καλόν, for own sake (1105a31) προαιρετόν

done for pleasure (incontinence) (1134a18)

{ done under duress (1110a4)
  done in necessity (1110a9)

{ for great good: praise 1110a2
  under great stress: pardon 1110a24
  via great evil: blame 1110a25
  for small good: blame 1110a27

in error { *re* law, of universal: wickedness (1110b28)
           in anger, inebriation (1111a24, 1135b20)
           of circumstances without regret (1110b18)

through error of particular circumstances { who
                                            whom
                                            what   } 1111a1
                                            with what
                                            why

force   no contribution from agent (1110a3)

voluntary

mixed

non voluntary

error

involuntary

CATEGORIES OF INJURIES IN THE *AE* A.8.

injuries			
	involuntary	in error through inhuman passion	inexcusable (1136a9)
		through fear, no error	unjust *per accidens* (1135b8)
		through reasonable error	misadventure, ἀδίκημα (1135b17)
	voluntary	through unreasonable error caused through negligence	inexcusable (?) (1135b18)
		through normal passion, with no error	ἀδίκημα, unjust *per se* (1135b23)
	premeditated (ἐκ προνοίας)	voluntarily, knowingly, after deliberation	makes a man unjust and wicked (1136b25)

Part Two

Purposive Choice

6. The Nature of Prohairesis

On the topic of προαίρεσις, or purposive choice,[1] the arguments of the *Eudemian* and *Nicomachean Ethics* are so closely parallel that it is most profitable to consider the two treatises together, at least in the chapters (*NE* 3.2, *EE* II.10) in which purposive choice is being defined and distinguished from similar or related mentalistic concepts. It would be a mistake, says the *NE*, to identify purpose with appetite, temper, will, or some form of belief. The *EE*, more systematic as usual, reveals the structure that produces these four candidates for identification with purpose: some say that purpose is either desire (ὄρεξις) or belief (δόξα)— certainly these two seem to accompany it—and if it is desire, then it must be one of the three forms of desire, volition, appetite, or temper (1225b21–26). These three forms of desire are the desires of the three parts of the Platonic tripartite soul: but those who are here criticised for misidentifying προαίρεσις can hardly include Plato himself (for the term is not a technical term of his, being used only once in the whole Platonic corpus, at *Parmenides* 143c; see Gauthier and Jolif, 1959, 189) but must be more recent Academic thinkers; unless we say that Plato is being criticised for *lack* of a psychological concept which is necessary and not superfluous since it cannot be identified with any of his own technical terms in this area. Aristotle briskly produces a battery of arguments to show that neither appetite, nor temper, nor volition possesses the attributes proper to purpose.

There are four arguments against the identification of pur-

[1] 'Purposive choice' seems to me the least misleading translation of προαίρεσις. Its clumsiness reflects the fact that no natural English concept corresponds to Aristotle's. I shall sometimes abbreviate to 'purpose' or 'choice'.

pose with appetite or temper: one drawn from animals, one from the continent and incontinent man, one from the relationship of these states to pleasure and pain, and one from the possibility of contradictory purposes. The first three arguments appear in both *Ethics*; the fourth only in the *Nicomachean*. (1) Irrational animals share appetite and temper but not purpose (1111b1, 1225b26–27). (2) Human beings, who possess both purpose and the other two states, may none the less form purposes without appetite or temper, says the *EE* (1125b28), having in mind perhaps the cold-blooded taking of decisions in matters where emotions are not aroused, or else the choice of a continent man to do something which he has no sensual desire to do; certainly, as the *EE* goes on to say, in the continent man there can be a sensual desire to do something, and a προαίρεσις *not* to do it: 'when under the influence of passion they do not choose to act, but remain firm' (1225b29). The *NE* says of the continent man that he acts προαιρούμενος but not ἐπιθυμῶν— there is, of course, in the continent man ἐπιθυμία (if he had no unruly desires he would not be continent, but fully virtuous); but there is no ἐπιθυμία to do that which he does in accordance with his purpose. Similarly, the *NE* says that the incontinent man acts ἐπιθυμῶν but not προαιρούμενος: this fits literally only the impetuous incontinent of book c; but even in the case of the weak-willed incontinent (1150b19), who *does* have a προαίρεσις, there is no προαίρεσις to do that which, following his appetite, he in fact does. (3) Sensual desire and anger are accompanied by pain (λύπη), says Aristotle in the *EE*: he means the felt dissatisfaction involved in states such as hunger, thirst and sexual arousal. The pursuit of a long-term purpose is not necessarily accompanied by any similar irritation. The *NE* makes the point about the relationship between sensual appetites and pleasure and pain in a different and rather puzzling manner:

> The object of appetite is the pleasant and the painful; the object of purpose is neither the painful nor the pleasant. (1111b16–18)

No doubt sensual appetite is an appetite for sensual pleasure;

but how can Aristotle say that the painful is an object of appetite? And why cannot pleasure be the object of purpose: is it not the object of the purpose in life of the intemperate man who always pursues, on principle, the present pleasure, according to book c (1146b22)? The answer to the first problem is suggested by the *EE* passage: the satisfaction of appetite is pleasantest when appetite makes further demands: eating when one is hungry, therefore, is both pleasant and in the broad sense painful.[1] The answer to the second must be that the intemperate man is precisely a man who makes pleasure his *good*: the pursuit of pleasure, he thinks, is the noble life. To choose something simply because it is pleasant, and not because of a policy about pleasure, is the act of an incontinent, not an intemperate man. The point is developed at length in a passage later in the *Eudemian Ethics* which concludes: 'Purpose concerns good and evil and apparent good and apparent evil: by nature pleasure is an apparent good, and pain an apparent evil' (1227b3–4). (4) The *NE* alone offers a further argument for the distinction:

Appetite can be contrary to purpose, but not appetite to appetite. (1111b15)

It seems to be a general contrast between sensual and intellectual desire (and not only the rather special intellectual desires that Aristotle calls 'purpose') that whereas one can have a volition that *p* be the case, and—even simultaneously—a volition that *p* not be the case, not both of these desires can be *felt*. Elsewhere (*Will, Freedom and Power*, 49), I questioned this statement of Aristotle's: cannot hunger and nausea be felt simultaneously? But it now appears to me that Aristotle (like Plato, *Republic* 440A) would regard nausea as an activity of the θυμός or temper: so that hunger and nausea felt simultaneously for the same object would not be a clash of appetite with appetite, but a clash of appetite with temper. The continent and incontinent man, of course, provide the constant example of the clash between appetite, or between temper, and purpose.[2]

---

[1] So Aspasius, explaining ἐπιθυμία καὶ ἐπίλυπον: πᾶν τὸ ἐνδεές he says καθὸ ἐνδεές, ἐπίλυπον· ἡ δὲ ἐπιθυμία ἐνδεές (*CAG* xix. 68).

[2] The second argument above is applied to both appetite and temper

F

From appetite and temper Aristotle now turns to the third kind of desire: volition. The same three arguments are offered in both *NE* and *EE* to show that purpose cannot be identified with volition (βούλησις, a broad term for intellectual wants and wishes).

(1) There is no προαίρεσις of things impossible, says the *NE* (1111b21), and if someone spoke of something impossible as his purpose, he would be thought a fool; but we can wish for impossible things, like immortality. The *EE* adds a further distinction and a further example. People *knowingly* wish for the impossible, he says, but no one takes something impossible for his purpose unless he is *mistaken* about its being impossible. Besides the wish to be immortal, the wish to be king over all men is given as an example of a wish impossible of fulfilment.[1]

(2) The second argument, in contrast, is given more fully in the *NE*. No one makes his purpose something which though within the realms of possibility is not in one's own power to do or not to do, says the *EE*: the *NE* makes explicit that such things can be the objects of wishing, and gives the example of the wish for the victory of a particular athlete or actor in a competition (1225b36; 1111b21-25).

(3) We wish for the end, and we choose the means, says the *NE* (1111b26-29), and the *EE* makes the same contrast: no one chooses the end, but chooses the means (1226a7-14); volition is especially for the end. Both treatises give health and happiness as instances of ends; only the *EE* instances the means to health (sitting and walking) and to happiness (making money and taking risks). More importantly, the *EE* goes on to make a general point which is absent from the *NE*: προαίρεσις involves

---

in the *EE*, but only to appetite in the *NE*. Aspasius comments (*CAG* xix.67): 'You can also find characters who are continent and incontinent of their anger (reading θυμοῦ at line 34), one of them acting in accordance with his purpose, and the other against it; so that by the same argument purpose is different not only from appetite but also from temper; but Aristotle thought it sufficient to show in the case of the continent and incontinent of appetite that appetite was different from purpose.'

[1] The example gives rise to speculation about the chronology of the treatises. Was it Alexander's dreams of universal dominion that suggested the addition of the example in the *EE*? Or did they cause its suppression in the *NE*?

two terms—it is always a case of choosing A for the sake of B, A being what is chosen (τί) and B being that for the sake of which the choice is made (τίνος ἕνεκα): a chooser has to be ready to answer both the question τί and the question τίνος ἕνεκα. This clarification offers the key to the solution of some difficulties raised by passages in which, in contrast to the present discussion, προαίρεσις seems to be linked with ends rather than with means (cf. 1227b38ff).

So προαίρεσις is not to be simply identified with any of the three kinds of desire: appetite, temper, or volition. Next it is to be shown that it is not to be identified with any kind of belief. It is easy to show that belief ranges much more widely than purpose: we can have beliefs, as we can have wishes, concerning eternal truths and necessary falsehoods (*NE* 1111b32), e.g. that the diagonal of a square is commensurate with its base (*EE* 1226a3). Moreover, beliefs, unlike purposes, are classified as true and false.

Perhaps no one, says the *NE*, would argue for a simple identification of purpose and belief. The more serious question is whether purpose may be a particular kind of belief (*NE* 1112a1): the belief, the *EE* suggests, that we should do, or refrain from doing, something in our power. Now there seem to be two reasons for refusing to identify a belief that one should ϕ with a purpose to ϕ. One is that beliefs of this kind may concern ends to be pursued as well as means to be taken; another is that it might be thought possible to have a belief that one should do something (an unpleasant duty, for instance) without acting on that belief or even intending to act on that belief. It is the first of these reasons which the *EE* develops, and the second which the *NE* develops.

The *EE* argument is explicitly parallel to the argument for refusing to identify προαίρεσις with volition. A man may think that he ought to be healthy or live a good life, just as he may wish to do either of these things; but the object of προαίρεσις is not these ends, but the means to them (1226a13–15).

The *NE* argument goes thus:

It is by our choices of good or bad things, and not by our beliefs, that our character is determined . . . it does not seem

that it is the same people who make the best choices and hold
the best opinions: some hold comparatively good opinions,
but because of depravity make the wrong choices. (1112a1–2,
8–10)

Two questions arise about this: first, surely character is determined not just by choice, but by acting upon choice;
secondly, who are the people who hold good opinions and make
bad choices, and how do they fit in to Aristotle's classification of
types of moral character?

It is not easy to answer the second question. The characters
here at issue can hardly be people who are wicked (μοχθηροί):
for Aristotle has told us only a few pages ago in the *NE* that the
wicked are in error about what they should do (1110b28); so
how can they be said to have good opinions? (No doubt there
is nothing to prevent a man having good opinions about geometry, and making bad moral choices: but in this section
Aristotle is talking about the identification of purpose with a
specific, and surely moral, set of opinions.) Nor can they be
incontinent people: for we have very recently been told that the
incontinent does not act προαιρούμενος (1111b14). There seems
to be no room for good δόξα and bad προαίρεσις in Aristotle's
Nicomachean system.

The *NE* offers three further arguments against the identification of προαίρεσις with belief: none of them raises any difficulty
other than a possible charge of superfluity. (1) We choose *to* do
or avoid things; we do not believe *to* anything, but believe *that*.
(2) Choice is praised for being choice of the right object, rather
than for being the right kind of choice; belief is praised not for
being about the right kind of object, but for being the right
kind of belief, *viz.* true. (3) Belief, unlike choice, is compatible
with a certain hesitancy of commitment (1112a2–14).

Both the *EE* and the *NE* pass immediately from the topic of
προαίρεσις to that of deliberation, because for both treatises
reference to deliberation enters into the definition of προαίρεσις.
The *NE* says that what is chosen is the subclass of voluntary
actions which is preceded by deliberation (1112a15); the *EE*
too says that the way to understand προαίρεσις is to relate it to
voluntariness, but it does not explain that this is because

προαιρετά are those voluntary actions preceded by deliberation or πρόνοια until after its delineation of the objects of deliberation (1226b32–36).

On the topic of deliberation, as on that of choice, there is very substantial agreement between the two *Ethics*; the topic will be treated later at length in the chapter on practical reasoning, so for the present it will be sufficient to bring out the main points of Aristotle's theory and to make explicit the links between deliberation and choice or purpose. In the course of marking off purpose from belief and from the three types of desire, Aristotle has delimited the field of choice: it cannot be of what is eternal or impossible, or of what, though possible, is not within the chooser's power; even within the range of the chooser's power it is restricted to means and not to ends: it is of means for the sake of ends. He now proceeds to show that the field of deliberation is delimited in exactly the same way, adding some further precision to the delimitation.

First, deliberation is concerned only with contingent matters: things, as the *EE* says, which can either be or not be the case (1226a1). So there is no deliberation about necessary truths (as that the diagonal is incommensurate with the side of the square, *NE* 112b23) or about necessary falsehoods (one cannot deliberate how to square the circle, *EE* 1226a30). But some contingent things are not fit matters for deliberation: solstices and sunrises and other phenomena in the course of nature which it is not in our power to produce (*NE* 1111a23–26, *EE* 1226a). If something is to be a subject of deliberation it must be something capable of being brought about by human action (it must be ἀνθρώπινον: *NE* 1112a28; it must be πρακτόν: *EE* 1226a30). The *NE* adds that we do not deliberate about things that happen by good luck, such as the finding of a treasure. This addition comes awkwardly: the difference between hitting on something by luck and hitting on it by deliberation is not a difference of subject matter: frequently what is achieved by luck is something that could have been done by deliberation when in fact no deliberation took place, as Aristotle himself points out, in a different context, in the disputed book в (1140a17–20). Certainly something can be the kind of thing that might happen by luck *and* be ἀνθρώπινον and πρακτόν·

finding a treasure is itself a case in point. Aristotle's awkward addition in the *NE* is due to his anxiety to relate his teaching on deliberation to the Platonic list of four cases: necessity, nature, chance and mind (cf. *Laws* x, 888Eff; Gauthier & Jolif, 1959, 199). The *EE* does not mention luck at this point: it devotes a lengthy section of its final book to the topic.

Not all human affairs, however, are topics of deliberation for everyone: only a small portion of them are within the sphere of influence of any given man. 'No Spartan deliberates about what form of government would be best for the Scythians,' says the *NE* (1112a29). 'We do not deliberate about the affairs of the Indians,' says the *EE* (1226a29), followed by the *MM* in its discussion of purpose (1189a20).[1] We deliberate, not about all πρακτά, but about those which are ἐφ' ἡμῖν (*NE* 1111a31, *EE* 1226a28, the latter as usual making precise that it is things which are in our power to do *or not to do*). But again, within this class, we must make two further distinctions: we must rule out the setting up of goals, and the blind following of rules, as cases of deliberation. Of the things that are in our power and which we bring about voluntarily, some are brought about as the result of reasoned reflection and some are not. Without reflection we may understand and obey a rule or command or resolution to do something or not to do it; and here 'we' includes children as well as adults (*EE* 1226b23–25). Instances of such unreflective following of rules can be found in routine arts such as orthography (*EE* 1226b1–2, *NE* 1112b2); as the *MM* says, no one deliberates how to write (i.e. spell) a name like Archicles. The *NE* gives another instance: the art of cookery: one does not deliberate whether the bread is baked or not; one just takes a look and decides whether to take it out of the oven (*NE* 1113a1–2). Of course one can make mistakes in spelling and in baking: but they aren't mistakes in reasoning, says Aristotle

---

[1] The Greek of *EE* 1226a29–31 should be punctuated as follows: διὸ οὐ βουλευόμεθα περὶ τῶν ἐν 'Ινδοῖς, οὐδὲ πῶς ἂν ὁ κύκλος τετραγωνισθείη— τὰ μὲν γὰρ οὐκ ἐφ'ἡμῖν, τὸ δ' ὅλως οὐ πρακτόν—ἀλλ' οὐδὲ περὶ τῶν ἐφ'ἡμῖν πρακτὸν περὶ ἁπάντων. The two clauses which follow are either misplaced in the MSS or are a maladroit parenthesis: they concern prohaireseis, not deliberation. On the possible implications of the examples in the *NE* and *EE* for the relative dating of the two treatises, see Kenny, 1978, 225.

in the *EE*, simply misdoings or misperceivings (1226b1). The area where there is scope for deliberation, the *NE* sums up, is the area where only rough generalisations are possible, where there is uncertainty about the outcome, and where there is no settled rule (1112b9).

Where two opinions are possible about how things can be done, there is scope for reasoning, and the reasoning, according to Aristotle, will always take a certain form: it will start from the end to be achieved by the action, and proceed to something which is in the agent's power. Because the reasoning starts from the end or goal to be achieved, this itself is not an object of deliberation in any given case. Hence, the field of deliberation is limited, as was the field of choice, to means and not to ends: to deliberate is to inquire into, to investigate, suitable means to a given end. προαίρεσις itself is the upshot of such an investigation: something προαιρετόν is ἐκ βουλῆς κριθέν (*NE* 1113a3); προαίρεσις is βουλευτική; that is to say, it is something whose origin and cause is a piece of deliberation (1226b19–20).

προαίρεσις, Aristotle insisted, was not to be identified with either desire or belief: but it is clearly very closely related to each. What is the precise relationship? About belief, the *NE* is cagey: 'Whether belief precedes or accompanies purpose is not to the point: we are not concerned with that, but only with whether purpose is to be identified with some form of belief' (1112a11–13). The only cognitive word it seems happy to use to describe προαίρεσις is 'judgment' (κριθέν, 1113a4; κρίναντες, a11). It is, however, prepared to allow 'desire' into the final definition of purpose: 'Purpose is deliberative desire of things in our power' (1113a12). The *EE* seems to regard προαίρεσις as being constituted both by a certain kind of desire and a certain kind of belief. It cannot be identified with desire and belief severally, or even conjointly (for a sudden desire to do something plus a sudden unreasoned belief that one should do it would not be a προαίρεσις), so 'it must be compounded of both, for both are found in a man choosing' (1226b5). What must be added is that the desire must be deliberative (i.e. caused by deliberation), as in the *NE*, and that the δόξα must be arrived at by reasoning (λογισμός) which will provide a final cause, a οὗ ἕνεκα or wherefore, for the purposed action. So we conclude 'προαίρεσις is not simply volition or simply belief, but belief plus desire when these follow as a conclusion from deliberation' (1227a1–4). Deliberation, then, is a process of reasoning which starts with desire and ends with desire: it leads from volition (βούλησις) to decision (προαίρεσις).

If such is the structure of προαίρεσις it will follow that whether a προαίρεσις is good or bad will depend on the goodness or badness of the initial volition, and on the correctness or incorrectness of the deliberative reasoning. In both *Ethics* Aristotle goes on to consider this question, but at this point the treatment of the topic, hitherto so similar in each treatise, begins to diverge.

The *NE* treatment is by far the briefer, and concentrates on the possibility of incorrect volition. Aristotle considers, in order to reject, two contrasting theories according to which incorrect volition would not in fact be a genuine possibility. On one view, that of Socrates and Plato in the *Gorgias* (468A–D), only what is good is ever genuinely willed: apparently incorrect volition, choice of evil, is not real volition (the phenomena are to be described as cases of mistaken belief, not wrong volition). On another view, that of sophists such as Protagoras, there can be no incorrect volition because it is for each man to choose his own good; there is no natural good, and nothing is good or bad but thinking makes it so. Aristotle disagrees with both these views:

> Absolutely and in truth the good is the object of volition; but for each person what appears to him good. That which is in truth the object of volition is the object of the good man's volition . . . the good man judges each class of things rightly, and the truth is what appears true to him. Each state of character differs in what it finds noble and pleasant, and perhaps the most important difference between the good man and others is that he sees the truth in each class of things, being as it were the standard and measure for each of them. (1113a25–33)

Having said that it is pleasure which makes the majority of men mistake apparent goods for real goods, the *NE* goes on to discuss the voluntariness or otherwise of the possession of mistaken conceptions of goodness (1114a31ff).

The *Eudemian Ethics* too draws the distinction between natural and apparent goods, in a passage which gives rise to some difficulties:

The end is by nature always a good and one about which people deliberate in particular, as a doctor may deliberate whether he is to give a drug, or the general where he is to pitch his camp; in these there is a good, an end, which is the best without qualification; but contrary to nature, and by perversion, not the good but only an apparent good may be the end. (1227a19–22)

Commentators and translators take the 'in particular' (κατὰ μέρος) to refer to the individual decisions referred to in the instances: Aristotle is saying that a drug, or a campsite, may be a particular good.[1] To me it seems more likely that here the expression 'κατὰ μέρος' refers to the particular goods which are the goals of these deliberations—health and victory, which are only parts of the good for man; and that these goods are being contrasted with the overall good for man, τὸ ἁπλῶς ἄριστον, the best end which is the goal of human action, described in *EE* 1 at 1218b11, which is the object of wisdom which controls the activities of the arts.[2] This goal, Aristotle is about to explain, is the mean or right amount of the particular natural goods.

Erroneous choice is possible, Aristotle explains, because βούλησις is not a faculty like sight which cannot be used except upon its proper object. One cannot see sounds or hear colours: but one can will what is bad, even though the object of volition is what is good. Volition, like knowledge, is something capable of abuse. Aristotle's language here smacks to a modern philosopher of a fanciful and futile mechanistic faculty psychology: but perhaps his point can be made in a more antiseptic way by saying that 'want' though it may involve 'thinking good' is not a

[1] Thus Solomon: 'Men deliberate about the particular questions, e.g. the doctor whether he is to give a drug, or the general where he is to pitch his camp'; Dirlmeier: 'κατὰ μέρος = καθ' ἕκαστον Gemeint sind die Mittel zum Ziel' (1969,299).

[2] Taking οἷς in οἷς ἀγαθὸν τὸ τέλος τὸ ἁπλῶς ἄριστον not as masculine (with Solomon and Rackham) but as neuter (with Dirlmeier) referring back to περὶ οὗ in line 19.

success-verb like 'see'. Like the *NE*, the *EE* blames pleasure and pain for the distortion of volition: indeed it identifies pleasure and pain with the apparent goods which may trick us into taking them for the genuine goods: 'We are so constituted that the pleasant appears good to the soul and the more pleasant better, while the painful appears bad and the more painful worse' (1227b1). What are the deceptive pains and pleasures he has in mind? They are the pleasures and pains which accompany and characterise the passions which provide the field for the operation of moral virtue (*EE* II.2, 1220b13): the feelings typical of fear, anger, lust and avarice. The virtues may be described indifferently as being concerned with the control of the passions, or with the management of pleasure and pain. Vicious choice results from the uncontrolled pursuit of the objects of the passions (honour, money, sensual pleasure or the like); virtuous choice results from the pursuit of the mean, the correct amount of these objects. The virtuous man wants the optimum, not the maximum, amount of the goods to which these passions are directed; and it is the wise man who knows what *is* the optimum amount in question. For Aristotle only the wise are virtuous and only the virtuous wise. To the relationship between virtue and wisdom the next chapters are devoted.

7. *Virtue and Purposive Choice in the* Eudemian Ethics

If virtue is a ἕξις προαιρετική, a disposition exercised in choice, and if a προαίρεσις consists in a choice of means to an end reached as a result of reasoning, then it seems that the exercise of virtue in a choice must involve both a good end and a correct piece of reasoning. A choice may go wrong either in being a mistaken choice of means to a good end, or a choice of means appropriate to a mistaken goal—or, indeed, in being a mistaken choice of means to a mistaken goal. The last chapter of *EE* II, from which the sentence just preceding was taken (1227b20–22), discusses in detail the relationship between virtues, goals, and means-end reasoning. The chapter is a difficult one, but it is of crucial importance to anyone interested in the relationship between Aristotle's ethical treatises. It has no real parallel in the *NE*, but it touches on themes which are the subject of extensive discussion in the *AE:* the relationship of virtue to continence (1227b15–19; cf. *AE* C, 1151b27–1152a3); the relationship of virtue to ends and means (1227b23–35; cf. *AE* B, 1144 a6–8, 1145a4–6); the distinction between virtue and another power of hitting on means (1227b38–49; cf. *AE* B, 1144a20–22); the comparison between practical and mathematical reasoning (1227b29–33; cf. *AE* B, 1142a28–30; *AE* C, 1151a16–18). But though the topics and the terminology of this chapter bear a close relation to those of the *AE*, there seem at first sight to be a number of inconsistencies in doctrine between the parallel treatments of the same topics. I shall try to show that the inconsistencies are only apparent, and that what we have in the present chapter is a preliminary crude statement of a position that will be developed and extended with the aid of further distinctions in books *AE* B and C.

'Let us say,' the chapter begins, 'whether what virtue does is to make the choice free from error and the end right, so as to be a choice for the sake of the proper end, or, as some think, to make the reasoning' (1227b12–14). The sentence seems clumsy, and appears to invite confusion. Surely, if the choice is to be free from error, then *both* the end *and* the reasoning must be right; and 'making the choice free from error' and 'making the end right' are by no means the same thing. As Aristotle himself immediately goes on to point this out, the whole ἀπορία, and not just the second option, must be meant to represent a confusion on the part of someone else. In fact, as we shall see, for the choice to be free from error we need virtue to make the end right and something else to make the reasoning right: thus the choice will be of the right means *for* the right end (both the τίνος and the ἕνεκα τίνος will be correct).

To the question 'Does virtue make the reasoning right?' any reader of the *NE* or *AE* will certainly expect the answer No. Right reasoning enters into the definition of virtue: but it appears more as a prerequisite than a product. But to the question 'What *does* make the reasoning right?' one expects the answer 'wisdom' (φρόνησις). Thus, in the *NE* virtue is defined as 'a state of character exercised in choice, lying in a mean relative to us, which is determined by reasoning such as a wise man would use' (1106b34), and we are told that correctness in morals is in accordance with wisdom (1178a18). In the *AE* we read 'Everyone nowadays, when defining virtue, after naming the state of character and its objects adds "that which is in accordance with right reasoning": and right reasoning is reasoning in accord with wisdom' (1144a2). We are therefore brought up short when in the present passage Aristotle goes on to say that it is continence that 'does this', i.e. makes the reasoning right. Is there a conflict between this and the *NE* and *AE* theory that it is wisdom which makes reasoning right? No: Aristotle is here following his regular practice of trying to squeeze the maximum of truth out of erroneous opinions, in the present case the erroneous opinion that it is moral virtue which makes reasoning right. The only sense in which virtue can be said to make reasoning right is that it prevents the corruption of reasoning by vice, a corruption whose possibility is emphasised by the *AE:* the end of practical reasoning, we are told in в (1144a33ff), is not apparent except to a good man, 'for wickedness perverts us and causes us to be deceived about the springs of action'. But, strictly speaking, an uncorrupted reason can remain present without virtue: a man who is merely continent will not have virtue (for he is not in perfect control of his desires), but he will not differ from a virtuous man in respect of cognitive processes of reasoning. This too is clearly stated in the *AE:*

> Both the continent man and the temperate man are such as to do nothing contrary to reason for the sake of bodily pleasures; but the former has, and the latter has not, evil desires. (1151b34–1152a2)

So, strictly speaking, it is continence, and not virtue, which makes reasoning right in the minimal sense of warding off the corruption of reason. And thus we reach the conclusion of the *EE* passage:

> What does this is continence: for it is this which preserves reason from corruption. But virtue and continence are two different things. We must speak later about them, since those who think that it is virtue that is responsible for right reasoning do so for this reason, namely, that continence is of this nature and continence is one of the things we praise.

They fail to recognise, that is, that there are praiseworthy states of character which fall short of virtue: the truth in their view is that there is a praiseworthy state of character which makes reasoning right in the minimal sense of preserving it from corruption. Thus interpreted, the view leaves room open for their to be another quality—wisdom—which has the positive, and not merely preservative, role in the provision of right reasoning.

We might query whether it is really in accord with the teaching of the *AE* to say that continence is required for the preservation of right reasoning. Does not *AE* allow that the incontinent man may have an impeccable προαίρεσις (1152a17)? An incontinent man may differ from a virtuous man at the level of

desire and of action, while being no different from him at the
level of reason. But this is true only of one kind of incontinent in
AE c: the weak-willed people who reason correctly but fail to
abide by their reasonings (ἀσθενεῖς), who are contrasted with
the headstrong incontinents (προπετεῖς) whose passions are so
strong that they are led astray by passion without deliberating
at all (1150b19ff). Consequently, it is only of the continent that
it can be said without exception that their reasoning is safe. The
further discussion of continence and incontinence in *AE* c is
exactly what is needed to give further precision to the brief
remarks here: and of course the forward reference in the
present passage fits perfectly the later discussion. Having referred forward to the future full discussion of the difference
between virtue and continence, Aristotle makes no further use
of the distinction in the present chapter: for what he now goes
on to say of ἀρετή is equally true of ἐγκράτεια: the virtuous man
and the continent man do not differ in their overall goal. To be
sure, their volitional-affective situation is not the same, since the
continent has room for unruly desires; but their overarching
goal, the one which controls the individual προαιρέσεις, is the
same. Even an ἀκρατής, in fact, does not differ in overarching
goal from a virtuous man; if he did, he would be not an ἀκρατής
but either a μοχθηρός (with an evil overarching goal) or an
ἄφρων (with no overarching goal at all) (1214b10). But as an
ἀκρατής may not have formed a προαίρεσις at all it is only the
target of the virtuous and continent that really need to be taken
into account.

Aristotle now reformulates his question:

Does virtue make the aim, or the means to the aim?

No doubt we must understand 'make' as 'make correct', as
above (so von Fragstein, 1974, 119, against Dirlmeier, 1969,
303), though there is no need, with Rackham, to interpolate an
ὀρθόν into the text. He opts for the first alternative *via* a rather
disconcerting argument. Correctness is caused either by virtue
or by reasoning. But there is no reasoning toward an end;
therefore the correctness of an end must be caused by virtue.
The argument is disconcerting because in the sentence 'Of all
correctness either reasoning or virtue is the cause' we have to

take cause first as material cause, then as a cause of some other kind. For λόγος, whether understood as a particular piece of reasoning or as the reasoning faculty in general, is of itself neutral between correctness and incorrectness: it is that of which correctness can be predicated; it is not, like virtue, either a formal or efficient cause of correctness. To use the vivid metaphor of *AE* B (1144a30), it is an eye: an eye which can be a good eye or an evil eye, depending on its ἕξις. No doubt what Aristotle must mean is that *correctness* in reasoning is a case of other correctnesses. For instance, correctness in reasoning may be a cause of the correctness of a conclusion. But the selection of a goal is not a conclusion of any argument, as Aristotle has already repeatedly insisted (1226b10, 1227a8): so the correctness of a goal is not a case of the correctness of a conclusion. If we assume, then, that virtue and correct reasoning can each be responsible for one, and no more than one, element in the correctness of a προαίρεσις, we can say that virtue makes the end correct but does not make the means correct. Any προαίρεσις is a προαίρεσις of A for the sake of B: reasoning is responsible for A's being the right thing to choose, and virtue is responsible for B's being the right thing to choose for the sake of:

> The end is the wherefore: for every purposive choice is a choice *of* something *for the sake of* something else. It is the mean which is the wherefore which virtue is the case of the purposive choice being for the sake of. Choice is not *of* the wherefore, but of the things done for the sake of it. Getting these right, the things which should be done for the sake of the end, is the task of another faculty; it is the correctness of the end of the purposive choice of which virtue is the cause. (1227b36–28a2)

The Greek is crabbed, compressed, and difficult, and almost all commentators feel obliged to amend at one or other point. The crucial second sentence reads in the manuscripts: οὗ μὲν οὖν ἕνεκα τὸ μέσον ἐστίν, οὗ αἰτία ἡ ἀρετὴ τὸ προαιρεῖσθαι οὗ ἕνεκα. Rackham, following Fritzsche and Susemihl, emends τό into τῷ and translates: 'The End is therefore the object for which the thing chosen is the mean, of which End goodness is the

cause by its act of choice', glossing thus: 'Virtue by choosing
the right means to achieve the End causes the End to be
realised.' But this is a confusion between 'mean' and 'means';
a confusion easier in English than in Greek, where the expressions τὰ πρὸς τὸ τέλος and τὸ μέσον do not at all resemble each
other. The golden mean is not the means, but the end, of an
Aristotelian virtuous choice: the choice is made in order to
realise in action the mean which is the best relative to us
(1220b28). Dirlmeier and von Fragstein retain the τὸ προαιρεῖσθαι, taking it in apposition to ἀρετή. Dirlmeier translates:
'Das "worumwillen" (man handelt) ist aber das Mittlere und
davon ist Ursache die Tugend, das Sich-entscheiden fur das
Worum-willen'; von Fragstein agrees with the overall sense of
this translation, while objecting that it makes it appear that the
οὗ ἕνεκα is the object of the προαίρεσις, something which Aristotle
immediately goes on to deny. These commentators are correct,
against Rackham, in regarding the mean as being the *end* of the
choice; this is confirmed when Aristotle says a little later that
vice makes purposive choice to be made for the sake of opposite
things (1228a5): for the sake of the excess and defect that are
contrasted with the mean (pleasure and pain, we have been
told at 1227a38ff, make the purpose erroneously move from
the mean to the greater or the less). But like Rackham they err
in thinking that Aristotle is telling us that virtue is the cause of
the mean, the cause of the mean's being realised in action. No
doubt it is: but what Aristotle here says is that virtue is the
cause of *the mean's being the goal of the choice*, of the mean's being
the οὗ ἕνεκα of the προαίρεσις.

If we must emend the τό of τὸ προαιρεῖσθαι, it should be
emended into τοῦ, not τῷ (1).[1] Aristotle's contorted sentence
gets built up thus. He wants to say:

Virtue is the cause of the choice's being for the sake of the
mean.

(ἡ ἀρετή ἐστιν αἰτία τοῦ προαιρεῖσθαι τοῦ μέσου ἕνεκα)

He then wishes to stress the importance of the mean, and so
brings it forward:

[1] Perhaps τό is in order, the construction being a rather clumsy accusa-
tive and infinitive after αἰτία, with the infinitive εἶναι left understood.

It is the mean that virtue is the cause of the choice's being for the sake of.

(τὸ μέσον ἐστίν, οὗ αἰτία ἡ ἀρετὴ τοῦ προαιρεῖσθαι οὗ ἕνεκα)

He then wishes to link the whole with the previous mention of the οὗ ἕνεκα or 'wherefore':

It is the mean which is the wherefore which virtue is the cause of the choice's being for the sake of.

(οὗ μὲν οὖν ἕνεκα τὸ μέσον ἐστίν, οὗ αἰτία ἡ ἀρετὴ τοῦ προαιρεῖσθαι οὗ ἕνεκα)

The final sentence of the quoted passage has also exercised commentators: almost all have felt obliged to delete the οὗ in the clause τοῦ δὲ τὸ τέλος ὀρθὸν εἶναι τῆς προαιρέσεως, οὗ ἡ ἀρετὴ αἰτία in order to make the text match what is undoubtedly the sense, namely, that virtue is the cause of the end of the purposive choice's being correct.[1] Little of importance hangs on the exact reading here, since the point has already been made unambiguously by Aristotle: more interesting is the statement that hitting on the things which are to be done for the sake of the end is the task of another faculty. Commentators, with the *AE* in mind, take this to be a reference to φρόνησις, or wisdom. This seems to be precipitate: Aristotle is deliberately being unspecific here, and φρόνησις strictly speaking is a ἕξις, not a δύναμις (1144a28–30). If we are to take the *EE* together with

---

[1] Perhaps a more economical change with the same effect would be to alter the initial τοῦ to τό, and taking ἐστιν as understood before οὗ.

Von Fragstein has made a gallant and ingenious attempt to defend the received text by varying the punctuation. He understands the passage thus: 'Purposive choice is not of the wherefore, but of the things for the sake of the wherefore. Getting these right, the things which should be done for the sake of the end, is the task of another faculty; but getting the end right (τοῦ δὲ τυγχάνειν τὸ τέλος ὀρθὸν εἶναι) is the task of the προαίρεσις; and it is that of which virtue is the cause.' The masculine οὗ does not, of course, refer back to προαίρεσις; on von Fragstein's view it refers to the whole clause, to the fact that the προαίρεσις can really achieve the rightness of the end: the προαίρεσις can only do this if virtue stands behind it. 'Die *orthotes* des Telos aber zu erweisen ist Sache der Proairesis, hinter der die Arete stehen muss' (1974, 121). This seems to clash too much with the repeated statement that προαίρεσις is not of the end; and it would surely require τὸ δὲ τοῦ τὸ τέλος ὀρθὸν εἶναι to match τὸ μὲν οὖν τυγχάνειν, or else a change of προαιρέσεως from genitive to nominative.

G

the *AE* we must say that in the present passage in talking of
λόγος and an ἄλλη δύναμις Aristotle is referring generically to
cognitive elements between which he will later carefully distinguish: at the present stage of the discussion he does not need
to cumber the text with yet premature distinctions between
δύναμις and ἕξις, between φρόνησις and δεινότης. There is a
precise parallel in his use of ἀρετή here. We have already noticed
that what he says about the σκοπός of ἀρετή from 1227b20ff applies with equal justice to ἐγκράτεια; but he does not in the present
passage make use of the distinction in spite of having explicitly
drawn attention to it immediately before. Similarly, he makes
no use of a distinction between natural virtue and moral virtue
strictly so called. There is no need yet to draw such a distinction,
since even in the *AE* when the distinction has been explicitly
drawn (after its foreshadowing in the *EE* at 1234a19) we are
told that either natural or acquired virtue is sufficient to give
one right opinion about the οὗ ἕνεκα, which is the principle of
moral action (1151a16–19). On the topic of the relation between virtue, choice, reasoning, ends and means, the teaching
of the final chapter of *EE* II is filled out, but not contradicted,
by the teaching of the disputed books; and to that we must now
turn.

8. *Reason, Desire and Choice in the* Aristotelian Ethics

The fullest and most systematic treatment of the relation between reason, desire, choice and conduct is given in the second chapter of the common book B:

> There are three things in the soul which control conduct and truth: sensation, intellect, and desire. Of these, sensation does not originate action; this is plain from the fact that brutes have sensation but do not share in conduct. (1139a18–20)

This passage is puzzling on a number of counts. First, what is the relationship between controlling conduct (being κυρία πράξεως) and originating conduct (being ἀρχὴ πράξεως)? Do the two expressions mean the same? If so, then Aristotle's point must be that sensation is a source not of conduct but of truth: it is κυρία ἀληθείας but not κυρία πράξεως; even in irrational animals sense-perception may be veridical. More likely, Aristotle is making a distinction between controlling and originating conduct, so that sensation while being κυρία πράξεως is not ἀρχὴ πράξεως. Certainly, in the account of the springs of human action in books B and C sensation is given a significant role (e.g. B 1142a27, 1143b5, 1147a26; and especially 1147b10 where we are told that a judgment about an object of sensation is κυρία τῶν πράξεων). What, then, is it to control without originating? Certainly, sensation *alone* cannot originate action; but this cannot be the distinction which Aristotle wishes to draw, for the same is true of intellect and desire. Certainly, again, sensation is not the beginning of the causal chain which leads to action; but this too cannot be the distinction, because προαίρεσις is called an ἀρχή of action though it itself has

ἀρχαί, namely reason and desire.[1] The sense of the distinction
between controlling and originating therefore remains obscure:
and the obscurity is compounded when we consider the argument which Aristotle offers to show that sensation does not
originate conduct. Irrational animals, he says, have sensation,
but they do not exhibit conduct. But do they not have desire,
no less than sensation—ἐπιθυμία is after all a form of ὄρεξις (*De
Anima* 433a25)—and so could not the same argument be used
to show that desire does not originate conduct?[2]

The solution to these problems is to realise that in this passage Aristotle is using ὄρεξις not in the broad sense in which it
includes even animal appetite, but in a narrow sense confined
to specifically human desire, such as the desire to lead a good
life (1139b4): a form of desire which can indeed be regarded as
a defining characteristic of a human being (1139b5). The sense
in which sensation is not an ἀρχή of conduct is that it is only in
the service of ὄρεξις that it has an effect on action. The same is
true of intellect: it too is not an ἀρχή of action except when
directed by desire. Aristotle's famous remark 'Thought by
itself moves nothing, but only practical thought aiming at an
end' is a precise parallel to his statement that sensation does not
originate conduct. The reason why προαίρεσις though not an
ultimate ἀρχή is yet an ἀρχή of conduct is that it itself contains
an element of ὄρεξις: it is, by definition, deliberative desire:

The origin of conduct—its efficient, not its final cause—is
purpose; and the origin of purpose is desire plus means-end
reasoning. (1139a31–33)

If the origin of conduct is purpose, does this mean that there
cannot be conduct where there is no purpose? Certainly,
animals, who lack purposes, have no share in conduct: but in the
lives of human beings, is an action disqualified as a πρᾶξις

[1] The distinction suggested here would be the converse of that at *EE* II.6,
1222a21, where κύριαι ἀρχαί are the sub-class of ἀρχαί which are first
movers.
[2] This point is insisted on by Gauthier and Jolif: 'On pourrait objecter
à Aristote qu'il en va de même du désir, que les animaux possèdent tout
comme la sensation, et il serait fort embarrassé pour répondre, car, comme
nous l'avons dit en commentant les sept premiers chapitres du livre III, il
n'a pas su dégager le concept de désir rationnel . . .' (1959,443)

unless it is the enactment of a προαίρεσις? No: involuntary actions, actions under duress, the actions of the incontinent are all πράξεις too (e.g. B, 1144a15–20; C, 1145b12, 1147a2; cf. *EE* II.11, 1228a14; *NE* 3.2 1111b13). So: purpose is not the only ἀρχή of conduct, but it is its ἀρχή *par excellence*: the most fully human action is prohairetic action; and no action can be a really good action unless it originates from a good προαίρεσις. Just as there can be πρᾶξις without προαίρεσις so too there can be προαίρεσις without πρᾶξις: such is the case with the incontinent man whose προαίρεσις is good but whose conduct is bad (1152a 17).

The reasoning which is here mentioned as the ἀρχή of προαίρεσις is the output of the intelligence (νοῦς) which was coupled with desire in the initial statement of the three things in the soul that controlled πρᾶξις and truth: the sequel shows that 'πρᾶξις and truth' are to be taken almost as a hendiadys: what we are inquiring into is the nature of *practical truth*: the truth of means-end reasoning (λόγος ἕνεκα τίνος):

> What affirmation and negation are in thinking, pursuit and avoidance are in desire: so that since moral virtue is a state which finds expression in purpose, and purpose is deliberative desire, therefore both the reasoning must be true and the desire right, if the purpose is to be good, and the latter must pursue just what the former asserts. This is the kind of thought and the kind of truth that is practical. (1139a21–27)

Throughout this chapter Aristotle uses the words 'intellect' (νοῦς), 'thought' (διάνοια), and 'reasoning' (λόγος) almost synonymously to refer to the cognitive faculty and its exercise.[1] The output, or ἔργον, of this faculty consists of positive and negative judgments (1139a21) which, if it is functioning well, are true and, if it is functioning ill, are false (1139a28). The faculty has been subdivided in the previous chapter into two elements: the scientific part (the ἐπιστημονικόν) whose field is necessary matters, and the deliberative part (the λογιστικόν, called after

---

[1] Thus νοῦς and διάνοια are used in hendiadys at 1139a32, recapitulated by διάνοια alone at a35; διάνοια of a21 is taken up by λόγος of a24.

the sense of λογίζεσθαι which is equivalent to βουλεύεσθαι) which concerns contingent matters. The deliberative part operates in two types of thinking: practical thinking, concerned with activities which are ends in themselves, and technical (ποιητική) thinking concerned with the productive arts. Both practical and technical thinking are instances of means-end reasoning in the broad sense (λόγος ἕνεκα τίνος) (1139a6–17, a27–31 1139b1–2). It is only this kind of reasoning which is an efficient cause of action (1138a37); and for the good operation[1] of this faculty mere truth is not enough: we need truth in concord with right desire.

What exactly is the relationship between desire, on the one hand, and pursuit and avoidance, on the other? Is it simply that pursuit and avoidance are the positive and negative species of the genus *desire*, as affirmation and denial are the positive and negative species of the genus *judgment*? And can a person's desire pursue an object without the person himself pursuing it: if a man has an ineffective desire for justice, being, say, incontinent, does his desire *pursue* justice in Aristotle's sense? The answers that we give to these two questions make a considerable difference to the way in which we understand the important passage quoted above, and in particular the requirement that 'the latter must pursue what the former asserts'. This requirement is itself doubly ambiguous. Is it governed by the clause 'if the purpose is to be good', being a further requirement for goodness of purpose in addition to truth of reasoning and rightness of desire; or is it something else which ought to be the case, (for some other reason) in addition to the goodness of the προαίρεσις—e.g. that the προαίρεσις should be acted on and not remain ineffective? And is 'the latter' which must pursue what reason asserts the προαίρεσις or the ὄρεξις? The feminine expression would fit either antecedent.

To unravel these difficulties, we must observe that Aristotle does not say that pursuit and avoidance are to desire as affirmation and denial are to *judgment*, but as affirmation and desire

---

[1] I take it that it is τὸ εὖ and not ἡ ἀλήθεια or τὸ ἔργον which is the tacit subject to be understood with the genitive διανοητικοῦ in the sentence τοῦ δὲ πρακτικοῦ καὶ διανοητικοῦ ἀλήθεια ὁμολόγως ἔχουσα τῇ ὀρέξει τῇ ὀρθῇ.

are to *thinking*. Now thinking (διάνοια) for Aristotle includes not
only belief and judgment, decisive cognitive attitudes (φάσις);
it includes also wondering and thinking out and the reflection
that may precede belief or judgment, prior to φάσις. Applying
the analogy to the non-cognitive part of the soul we can say
that ὄρεξις includes the states and processes which lead up to
the formulation of decisive desires as well as the specific pro-
and con-attitudes that are the outcome of these preliminaries.
Thus, a general desire to be just, or courageous, or learned, may,
as a result of deliberation, find expression in a decision to take
a particular course of action: of pursuit or avoidance. Pursuit
and avoidance, therefore, are to desire in general as the specific
and decisive is to the vague and variously realisable. προαίρεσις,
by contrast with βούλησις, is the decisive type of ὄρεξις: it is
itself a decision to act (a pursuit) or to refrain from acting (an
avoidance). It is a mental state which finds expression, if
dramatised, in utterances such as 'Pursue this', 'Avoid that'
(cf. c.3, 1147a27, 34). As the instance just quoted from the
discussion of the incontinent man shows, it is possible for
προαίρεσις to say 'Pursue this' without the agent actually pursuing it. The requirement that 'the latter should pursue what
the former asserts' is not a requirement for the purpose's being a
good one: it is a description of what there must be if there is to
be a προαίρεσις at all.[1] The reasoning, the λόγος, must reach a
conclusion in the form of a φάσις, and the desire, the ὄρεξις,
must reach a decision in the form of a δίωξις, or there is not a
προαίρεσις, which, as we recall from *EE* 1227a4–5, is opinion

---

[1] This is well put by Greenwood (1909, 175). 'The harmony of reason
with appetite is not the same thing as the goodness of either ... For *every*
προαίρεσις, good or bad, it is necessary that the reason and the appetite
should be concerned with the same object: otherwise there is merely an
opinion, right or wrong, about one thing, and a desire, right or wrong, about
another, and no προαίρεσις can occur. For *good* προαίρεσις it is necessary
that both reason and desire should be good in themselves.' But Greenwood's
further discussion of 'the harmony of reason with appetite' is vitiated by an
equivocation in his use of 'harmony', which sometimes means reason and
desire's being concerned with the same object, and sometimes means their
both being good, or both being bad, as the case may be. Greenwood does
not realise that the true λόγος is not the φάσις itself, but the argument leading
up to it.

plus ὄρεξις reached as a conclusion of deliberation. Aristotle is not simply ruling out a perverse attribution of purpose to a man who has a good desire for justice, and a true λόγος about house-building: of course the reasoning and desire have to concern the same topic. But he is making the stronger point that the φάσις which is the conclusion of the λόγος contribution to deliberation, and the δίωξις which is the upshot of the ὄρεξις contribution to it, are one and the same thing. For προαίρεσις is at one and the same time desiderative thought and deliberative desire.

The λόγος which must be ἀληθής is the λόγος ἕνεκά τίνος, the λόγος which presents the course of the deliberation in such a way as to explain the reason for the decision. I shall argue later that it has the broad features of the 'practical syllogisms' which are to be found scattered through the works of Aristotle and his commentators. For the moment it is only necessary to point out that ἀληθής, as a predicate of λόγος when that means an argument, must mean 'sound', rather than simply 'true'. ἀλήθεια is correctness of λόγος; and the correctness of arguments is soundness, which includes both truth of premises and validity of form. We shall later inquire what validity of form might be in practical reasoning. Already we can observe that if the conclusion of a piece of practical reasoning has the imperative form 'Pursue this' or 'Avoid that' it is not something which can itself be straightforwardly described as true or false.

Practical truth is the particular form of ἀλήθεια which belongs to a λόγος ἕνεκά τίνος which is the output of the διάνοια πρακτική. There can be practical truth in the reasonings of an evil man. An intemperate man, devoting his life to the unremitting search for sensual pleasure, may have an excellent understanding of the nature of his goal and show exquisite intelligence and perception in his pursuit of it: his λόγος will be ἀληθής, but it will not be an example of the good operation of practical reason, because its truth is not in harmony with right desire.

'Goodness' is the genus of which 'true' and 'right' are species: goodness in logic is truth, goodness in desire is rightness: and a desire is right if it is a desire *for* the right thing. (Cf., in the particular case of προαίρεσις, *NE* 3.2, 1112a6.) Clearly, a desire can be right only if it is a desire for a good: but there are various kinds of goods. There are, in the first instance, the goods which are pursued by the particular arts and skills: health, wealth, victory, conviction, for example, pursued professionally by the doctor, the entrepreneur, the general, the orator. Decisions reached in the pursuit of these goals by sound reasoning are surely candidates for being instances of good προαιρέσεις: and indeed in the treatments of προαίρεσις in *NE* 3 and *EE* II it is such decisions which have standardly provided illustrations of the concept—the decision to walk or rest in order to promote one's health (*NE* 3, 1111b27; *EE* II, 1226a9), the decision how to treat a patient or where to pitch camp (*EE* II, 1227a20). The deliberations leading to these decisions would be, in the terminology of book B, operations of the διάνοια ποιητική, the technical reason: and Aristotle now makes further precisions about its role:

> Practical thought governs productive thought: for whoever produces something produces for the sake of an end: the product itself is not an end in an unqualified sense, but an end only in a particular relation and of a particular craftsman. A deed done, however, *is* an end in an unqualified sense: for good conduct is an end, and desire is aimed at that. (1139b1–4)

Every productive skill has an end-product (which need not be a concrete product, such as a house, but may be conditions such as health, conviction, or public order), an end product which is distinct from the activity which is the exercise of the skill. This product is itself an end, but it is always, in Aristotle's view, sought for the sake of some further end.[1] When Aristotle says that a product such as health is not an end ἁπλῶς, but an end πρός τι, does he mean that it is an end only in comparison with the means which lead up to it (e.g. slimming and exercise), or

---

[1] It is not clear whether the ἕνεκά του in the sentence ἕνεκα γάρ του ποιεῖ πᾶς ὁ ποιῶν refers to the end-product or to the further end. I incline to the former interpretation, which makes the reference to reasoning which is ἕνεκά του καὶ ποιητική balance the reasoning which is ἕνεκά του καὶ πρακτική in line 1139a37. Most commentators take the second interpretation, which makes Aristotle say already what he is going on to say in the second clause, that the product is not an end ἁπλῶς.

does he mean that it is an end which is a means towards a
further end (i.e. happiness)? The expression πρός τι can be
taken in either sense; and it does not much matter how we take
it in the present passage since both senses express thoughts with
which Aristotle would agree. Why does Aristotle say that such
and end is an end τινος: an end of a particular individual?[1]
Surely all ends, including εὐπραξία, are ends pursued by individuals? The contrast Aristotle has in mind is between the end
pursued by an individual *qua* human being (that is an end without qualification) and the end pursued by an individual *qua*
general, orator, or doctor, which is an end τινος. This is how
we are to reconcile the statement made here that the ends of
technical disciplines are pursued for the sake of further ends
with the statements in both the *NE* and the *EE* that doctors and
orators and generals do not deliberate about their ends: they
may deliberate about the ends of their crafts *qua* human beings,
but they do not deliberate about them *qua* craftsmen.[2] εὐπραξία,
however, or good conduct, requires qualification: it is not something which is desired for the sake of a further end, nor which
can itself be chosen as a result of deliberation at any level.[3]

We are now in a position to consider one of the most difficult
sentences in the chapter:

Purpose cannot exist without intellect and thought nor without moral character; for good conduct and its opposite in the

[1] Gauthier translates 'fin de tel individu'; surely rightly, against Greenwood, Ostwald, and Ross, who take the τινος to refer to an operation
not a person. The interpretation suggested above make the two translations
come to the same as each other.

[2] This is already hinted at in the obscure passage *EE* II.10, 1227a21,
discussed above at p. 79. The architectonic relation between the particular
crafts and the discipline which concerns the whole good of man is the theme
of the first section of *NE* I and the last section of *EE* I (1094a1–1094b11;
1218b11–27), and both *NE* and *EE* draw the distinction between activities
which have products and those which are ends in themselves, though without the ποίησις/πρᾶξις distinction (1094a3–5; 1219a13–16).

[3] The word εὐπραξία is the bane of translators: it means 'to act well'
'to do well' 'to do good' 'to do good deeds', but all these expressions like
'good conduct' have distracting overtones in English. It is meant to express the active nature of happiness as Aristotle conceives it. Perhaps 'a well-
spent life' is as close a translation as any.

sphere of conduct cannot exist without intellect and moral character.

The statement that purpose cannot exist without intellect and thought is unproblematic and is an obvious consequence of Aristotle's repeated definition of προαίρεσις: but why does he say that it cannot exist without moral character? The Greek expression ἠθικὴ ἕξις usually means one of the virtues or vices described in *NE* 3 and 4 and *EE* III: to have a ἕξις of this kind, according to *NE* 2, you have to do the appropriate actions knowingly, choosing them for their own sake, and with a firm and unchangeable character (1105a31–33). προαίρεσις appears here only as one among several necessary conditions, rather than as a sufficient condition, of moral character. Moreover, must there not be many choices which fulfil the definition of προαίρεσις as a conclusion of deliberation which are performed by human beings who do not fulfil Aristotle's rather strict conditions for being ἀγαθός or μοχθηρός? Aristotle concedes that an incontinent man may deliberate successfully to achieve what he proposes (1142b19–20). A person on a diet, let us say, succumbs to temptation and bakes a delicious but fattening cake. Are not the results of the incontinent cook's deliberations ('So I'll put in a pound of sugar') cases of προαίρεσις? Yet the incontinent is, by definition, not quite vicious, and far from virtuous.

If Aristotle's assertion here is puzzling, the argument he offers for it is even more puzzling. The argument seems to go: you cannot have εὐπραξία without thought and character; you cannot have εὐπραξία without προαίρεσις; so you cannot have προαίρεσις without thought and character. The formal invalidity of this argument is obvious; and once again the incontinent provides a counterexample by verifying the premise (he does not live well because he lacks the character to put his προαίρεσις into action) and falsifying the conclusion (he has a good προαίρεσις but not a good character). Greenwood, one of the most patient of commentators, despaired of the passage and declared it an interpolation. 'If obvious and complete inappropriateness and logical unsoundness is warrant enough for bracketing a passage,' he wrote, 'the words ... ought to be bracketed. For these words add nothing to the argument of the previous sentence. Moreover they appear to try to prove one statement by another that is logically posterior to it' (1909, 176).[1]

The first step to unravelling these puzzles is one taken by Greenwood himself: it is to take ἕξις in ἠθικὴ ἕξις, and ἦθος, the two expressions translated 'moral character', to mean *any* condition of the affective part of the soul, and not only the rather strictly defined conditions of virtue and vice. In this broad sense of ἕξις, ἀκρασία too is a ἕξις. It might be thought that to take the expression in this sense is to trivialise the thesis: no doubt everyone is always in some ἕξις or other, and so the thesis that there cannot be προαίρεσις without moral character is as vacuous as the thesis that there cannot be προαίρεσις without breathing. But Aristotle's point is that a person's προαίρεσις will always *reveal* his moral character: trace a man's practical reasoning up to the end which he sets himself, and you will discover whether he is virtuous, vicious, brutish, foolish, incontinent or whatever.

Consider, for instance, the general's decision where to pitch his camp. This will be guided by his professional aim to win a victory in battle. But we can ask further why he wants to win a victory: is it to defend his country from the threat of conquest, to further his own military or political career, or is it in the hope of acquiring sufficient plunder to enable him to retire to a life of Lucullan luxury? The answer to this question will tell us what his ideal of a good life is, how he conceives εὐπραξία.

The incontinent person does not really present a counter-instance to Aristotle's generalisation about the relation between purpose and character, if we interpret character broadly. An incontinent action on impulse presents no difficulty, since there is no deliberation involved and so no purpose even according to the broad definition as 'decision after deliberation'. But even where an incontinent person deliberates how to produce pleasure (whether using a technical skill, like that of a pastry-

---

[1] Gauthier defends the passage against Greenwood: but he has nothing to say in reply to Greenwood's criticism of the fallaciousness of the argument except 'Dieu merci, Aristote n'est pas si intrepidement déductif' (1959, 44).

cook, or mere *ad hoc* ingenuity) there is no exception to the rule that inquiry into προαίρεσις will reveal character. We ask for the reason of the action, and are told that it will produce pleasure. We then ask whether the agent has a general policy of pursuing pleasure. If so, he is an intemperate man, and we know his character; if not, and he gives no reason for pursuing pleasure in the present instance, he is an incontinent man, and again we know his character; while if he gives some other reason (e.g. 'even the hardest-working politician needs a break sometimes') that in turn will reveal something about his picture of a well-spent life.[1]

There seems to me no reason to deny that the decisions of an incontinent man exercising skill are προαίρεσεις. Clearly they are by the standards of *NE* 3 and *EE* II: but they need not be ruled out by the further precisions of book B. But we must say that just as health, victory, and delicious cooking are not ends ἁπλῶς, so the decisions taken as a result of deliberations about how to produce these ends are not προαίρεσις ἁπλῶς. The incontinent man has no προαίρεσις to produce pleasure: if he did he would be not incontinent but intemperate; but this does not rule out his having a προαίρεσις to, e.g., add a touch of garlic for the sake of making a dish more pleasant.[2]

The incontinent man does have a προαίρεσις—an ineffective one—to be temperate. So that if he also makes deliberative decisions in the pursuit of pleasure, he has conflicting purposes. This complicates the simple picture of incontinence as a conflict between reason and desire; but only in a way which easily fits Aristotle's discussion of incontinence in book C and which

[1] I am here modifying an account which I developed at greater length in *Will, Freedom and Power* (17–18). The basic lines of that account seem to me correct, but in writing it I was too anxious to bring B into accord with the classification of goals in *NE* I, and left no room for deliberations whose goals are the ἁπλῶς ἀγαθά of *EE* VIII.

[2] I here take issue with Professor Anscombe who writes: 'Book VI teaches us, as I think we might not have realised from book III, that there is no such thing as a 'choice' which is *only* technical . . . There is always, on Aristotle's view, another 'choice' behind a technical or purely executive one' (1965, 147). My interpretation is only slightly different from hers, but makes the reconciliation between the *NE/EE* treatment and the *AE* treatment of προαίρεσις easier.

accords with everyday experience. There can also surely be
cases where someone uses deliberation in the pursuit of pleasure
without having either an overall policy of pursuing pleasure
or an overall resolve to live a temperate life. And in general,
it seems possible to take decisions in aid of particular short-
term goals without having any thought-out overall policy of how
to spend one's life. It is a matter of dispute whether Aristotle
admitted this possibility in the *NE*.[1] In the *EE* he clearly did,
and he has a name for the moral character that such a situation
reveals: ἀφροσύνη, or folly (1.2; 1214b11).

We can now see why it is that Aristotle can offer the fact that
εὐπραξία involves both thought and character as a reason for
saying that purpose involves both thought and character. It is
because εὐπραξία is the end of προαίρεσις *par excellence*.[2] To aim
at εὐπραξία one must have a grasp of the intellectual and moral
characteristics involved in living a good life: one must know
what kind of person one wants to be. This knowledge is part of
the λόγος which is involved in purpose; and since *wanting to be a
certain kind of person* is itself a morally significant character trait,
purpose involves character also. So Aristotle does have, and
does offer, good reason for his conclusion that there can be no
purpose (in the strict sense) without intellect and thought nor
without character (in the broad sense).[3]

---

[1] At *NE* 1.12, 1102a2 Aristotle says that we all do everything else for
the sake of happiness; and at 1094a19 he appears to offer a (fallacious)
argument to the effect that there is some single aim at which all our choices
aim. I have in the past (1965) defended Aristotle against the charge of
fallacy here; but I am no longer so convinced that the *NE* is thus defensible.
Certainly, 1102a2, on the face of it, seems to conflict with the account of the
incontinent man given in the *AE*.

[2] As Aristotle says at 1139b4. A bad man, of course, no less than a good
one, aims at εὐπραξία; but as his view of what is a good life is misguided, it
will turn out in practice not a good life but a bad one: it will be τὸ ἐνάντιον
ἐν πράξει.

[3] In the order of my exposition of B.2 I have constantly departed from
Aristotle's own order. The way to read the chapter which best brings out
the logical structure of the argument seems to me thus:

   (i) Τρία δή ἐστιν ... κοινωνεῖν, 1139a17–20
   (ii) πράξεως μὲν οὖν ἀρχή ... λόγος ἕνεκά τίνος, 1139a30–32
   (iii) διὸ ἢ ὀρεκτικὸς νοῦς ... ἄνθρωπος, 1139b4–5
   (iv) ἔστι δ' ὅπερ ... ὀρέξει τῇ ὀρθῇ, 1139a21–31

(v) διάνοια δι' αὐτή ... ὄρεξις τούτου, 1139a35–b4
(vi) διὸ οὐτ' ... οὐκ ἔστιν, 1139a33–35.

This is almost the same as the order in which Greenwood proposed that the text should be read, except that he proposed that (vi) should be read after (ii). The order I propose has the merit that the discussion of the conditions for προαίρεσις as such are completed before the question what makes a προαίρεσις good or bad is raised. Like all commentators I regard 1139b5–11 as a footnote: this remark that there can be no choice, or deliberation, concerning what is past would be better in place in *NE* 3 or *EE* II. As Gauthier and Jolif say, 'c'est un exemple frappant de l'état d'inachèvement et de désordre dans lequel nous est parvenu le livre VI'. But I would say of my arrangement, as Stewart and Greenwood said of theirs, 'it is offered, not as a reconstruction of the text as it may have originally stood, but as an attempt to make the meaning of the passage, as we now have it, clearer'.

9. Choice, Virtue and Wisdom in the Aristotelian Ethics

At several points in the *AE* Aristotle addresses himself to the question raised in the last chapter of *EE* II, whether virtue makes the end or the means correct. Having established that φρόνησις, or wisdom, is the virtue of the deliberative or ratiocinative part of the soul (the λογιστικόν), he inquires in chapter 12 of book B whether it has any utility. Among the answers he gives is the following:

> What we are to do is achieved only in accordance with wisdom as well as with moral virtue; for virtue makes the goal aimed at correct, and wisdom makes the means correct. (1144a6–10)

Here wisdom seems to be offered as filling the role of the other faculty mentioned in *EE* II at 1227b39: but a few lines later further precision is added:

> Virtue makes the choice right, but the things that fall to be done for the sake of it are not the province of virtue but of a different faculty. We must pause to make these matters clearer. There is a faculty which is called intelligence: it is the power to hit upon and perform the steps which lead to the goal we have set ourselves.[1] If the goal is a noble one, then the intelligence is laudible; if not, it is cunning ... Wisdom is not identical with this faculty but it is impossible without it. (1144a20–29)

[1] There is no need to amend the reading of all the manuscripts, τυγχάνειν αὐτῶν, to τυγχάνειν αὐτοῦ with Bywater. The MS reading no doubt suffers from a certain redundancy; but the form of expression accords exactly with the parallel in *EE* II at 1227b39.

Aristotle then goes on to describe intelligence as 'the eye of the soul': it acquires the ἕξις of wisdom only through the presence of virtue.

How can Aristotle say that virtue makes the choice right, when he has made clear earlier that for good choice is needed not only the right desire which is the output of virtue, but also the right reasoning which is the exercise of wisdom? (B.2, 1139a25; cf. 1144b23). The preceding context provides the answer: the rightness which Aristotle here has in mind is that of being a choice made for the right end. He is answering the objection that wisdom is useless: the claim that knowing what is good and fine and just for man will not make anyone more virtuous, any more than a knowledge of medicine makes a man healthier. In reply, Aristotle begins by conceding that one can do just and moral actions without possessing either virtue or wisdom. Someone may pay his debts not out of love of justice but out of fear of going to prison (1144a13–16; this is just *per accidens*, 1135b6). But such action only makes a man virtuous if he does it out of choice, for its own sake, because it is just. It is *this* rightness of choice, the choice being of the just action for its own sake, that virtue contributes.[1]

The overall answer to the objection which Aristotle offers is the proof that virtue and wisdom are not separable in the way that health is separable from a knowledge of medicine. The first half of the proof, which is the one from which the quoted passage is taken, is the proof that wisdom is impossible without virtue: there may be intelligence without virtue, but not wisdom. Even intelligence devoted to the service of good ends, though laudable, does not amount to wisdom, for Aristotle: for it can be present in an incontinent man, who has a good προαίρεσις but does not act on it; and an incontinent man cannot be regarded as wise (c.10, 1152a6–17).

The second half of the proof establishes that real virtue is impossible without wisdom. To show this, Aristotle must first distinguish between natural and acquired virtue. Even as children, and without, therefore, having acquired wisdom, we can feel drawn to justice, temperance and courage; but without wisdom

---

[1] If 1144a21 is not to clash with 1144a25, we must take ἐκείνης in line 21 to refer back to ἀρετή, not to προαίρεσις.

H

we do not possess these virtues strictly so called, and our tendency towards them may even be positively harmful, like the
strength of a blind man. Only wisdom will turn these naturally
virtuous tendencies into real virtues:

> Just as in the cognitive part of our soul there are two types,
> intelligence and wisdom, so in the moral part there are two
> types of virtue, one natural and one strictly so called; the
> latter type is impossible without wisdom. (1144b14–16)

It is not enough to say that virtue is determined by the right
reasoning of a wise man, as one might say that medical treatment is determined by the instructions of a doctor (cf. 1138b30):
'virtue is not just a state determined by right reasoning, but a
state accompanied by right reasoning: and right reasoning about
these matters is wisdom' (1144b28). The wise instructions and
their virtuous execution must both originate and be united in
the same person. Thus virtue without wisdom is as impossible
as wisdom without virtue (1144b30–32). Summing up his reply
to the objector Aristotle concludes:

> No choice will be right without both wisdom and virtue. For
> the one makes one perform the acts leading to the end, and
> the other the end.

The second of these two sentences is cryptically concise: ἡ μὲν
γὰρ τὸ τέλος ἡ δὲ τὰ πρὸς τὸ τέλος ποιεῖ πράττειν. The Greek leaves
open two questions: first, which is 'the one' and which is 'the
other'; secondly, what verb are we to supply to take 'the end'
as its object? Given the order of the Greek, it would be slightly
more natural to take ἡ μέν, which is concerned with the end, as
being wisdom, and ἡ δέ, which makes us take the steps to the end,
as being virtue. The verb with τὸ τέλος can hardly be ποιεῖ
πράττειν: the expression πράττειν τὸ τέλος, 'to perform the end',
would be without parallel in Aristotle. Given that the sentence
is clearly a summary of chapters 12 and 13, no doubt we must
take ἡ μέν as referring to virtue and ἡ δέ as referring to wisdom;
such chiastic use of μέν and δέ is not uncommon in the disputed
books (e.g. 1151a6, 1150b19). We shall then have to supply

some expression such as ποιεῖ ὀρθόν to be understood before τέλος; and we shall have to understand that wisdom makes one *perform* the means (and not just discover or realise them) in the rather roundabout sense that if there is wisdom present then there must be true virtue too, and not just incontinent goodwill, so that the steps necessary will actually be taken and not remain at the level of ineffective προαίρεσις.

This is all rather clumsy, and it would indeed be possible to take the sentence, considered apart from its immediate context, in a different manner: as saying that wisdom makes one rightly judge the end (supplying some expression such as ὑπολαμβάνει ὀρθῶς before τὸ τέλος), and that virtue makes one actually carry out the steps which wisdom's right appreciation of the end suggests as appropriate means. Whether or not the present passage is so to be taken, the doctrine just enunciated is certainly good Aristotelian theory, as we can see if we look at the passage a few pages earlier in which there is a discussion of εὐβουλία, excellence in deliberation.

εὐβουλία, Aristotle says, is not to be identified with knowledge or belief: for deliberation is a process of inquiry, whereas both knowledge and belief are settled states (1142b1–2, 11, 14). Nor is it correctness of knowledge or belief: for knowledge cannot be mistaken, and there can only be correctness where there can also be mistake; and correctness in the case of belief is truth (1142b6–11). It is a kind of correctness, but if we want to say what it is correctness in we shall have to use a more general cognitive word such as λόγος or διάνοια, something broad enough to include mental states and attitudes of an inquiring rather than a decided kind:[1] as its name suggests it is correctness of βουλή, or deliberation. But not all correct βουλή is altogether *good* βουλή, deserving the name of εὐβουλία: a wicked or incontinent man may deliberate successfully, if he is clever enough,[2] in pursuit of his evil goals. It must be correct reason-

---

[1] It is thus that I understand αὕτη (*sc.* διάνοια) γὰρ οὔπω φάσις taking the οὔπω in a logical rather than a temporal sense, as meaning not that διάνοια is essentially a state of indecision (a theory for which I know of no support elsewhere) but that διάνοια is not essentially a state of decision.

[2] Accepting Ross's brilliant emendation εἰ δεινός for ἰδεῖν in the sentence ὃ προτίθεται ἰδεῖν ἐκ τοῦ λογισμοῦ τεύξεται at 1142b19.

ing in pursuit of good goals. Moreover it must not be merely accidentally correct reasoning which produces a correct result by unsound arguments: it must be valid reasoning from true premises.[1] Any reasoning which leads by sound arguments, in a reasonable time, to a good end will be an instance of εὐβουλία: but different good ends will be related to different kinds of εὐβουλία. There will be particular forms of εὐβουλία in the pursuit of particular ends: medical εὐβουλία in pursuit of health, for instance. εὐβουλία *par excellence*, εὐβουλία without qualification, will be that exercised in pursuit of the *end* par excellence, what is unqualifiedly 'the end':

> If, then, it is characteristic of wise men to have deliberated well, excellence in deliberation will be correctness in relation to what conduces to the end of which wisdom is the true apprehension. (1142b31–33)

There has been much controversy about the correct way to read this final sentence of the chapter. The natural way to understand the expression ὀρθότης ἡ κατὰ τὸ σύμφερον πρὸς τὸ τέλος, οὗ ἡ φρόνησις ἀληθὴς ὑπόληψίς ἐστιν is that wisdom is the true apprehension of a certain end, taking τέλος as the antecedent of the relative οὗ. This too is what is suggested by the build-up of the chapter. There are various εὐβούλιαι for various ends: we must then ask *what* is the end of εὐβουλία ἁπλῶς; and the final sentence gives us the answer: the end of which φρόνησις is the true apprehension.

Some scholars, however, have argued that the correct antecendent of the relative οὗ is the expression τὸ σύμφερον πρὸς τὸ τέλος, so that Aristotle would be saying that wisdom is a true apprehension of what conduces to the end. This would make the passage more closely parallel with the introduction to the discussion of wisdom in the preceding chapter:

> It is commonly thought to be characteristic of a wise man to be able to deliberate well about what is good and expedient for himself, not in some particular respect, e.g. about what

[1] Aristotle has only the single word ἀληθής to do duty for 'valid', 'true' and 'sound'.

sort of things conduce to health or strength, but about what sort of things conduce to the good life in general. (1140a25–28)

Pointing to passages such as 1141b15, where we are told that wisdom is concerned with particulars, some have argued that the province of wisdom, for Aristotle, is concerned only with the means to the end, and in no way with the end itself.

Now it is true that wisdom, being a cognitive and not an affective faculty, is not that which, in Aristotle's system, desires, pursues, or aims at any end, or at the good life in particular. But the successful pursuit of the good life involves not only an effective desire for it, but also a correct appreciation of its nature: of what constitutes a good life, and of how it is to be achieved. Someone who pursues the good life under the mistaken belief that it is a life of successive momentary pleasures, or who pursues justice under the mistaken belief that it consists in taking from each according to his ability and giving to each according to his need, will in a sense be aiming at the correct end; but his misconception of the nature of the end will render his pursuit vain and vicious.

Wisdom, then, though it does not *pursue* the end, is concerned with the end in that it includes a correct appreciation of it. The way in which this relates to the virtuous action of the good man is this: it provides the starting point and ultimate basis of his practical reasoning, and his practical reasoning in its turn is the basis of his virtuous action. In order to complete our consideration between virtue and wisdom, therefore, we must wait until we have investigated Aristotle's theory of practical reasoning and its relation to action.

Part Three

Practical Reasoning

10. *Practical, Technical and Ethical Syllogisms*

Many of the traditional English expressions for Aristotelian concepts are misleading. 'Voluntary' and 'involuntary', 'pain' and 'pleasure' and other terms, as we have seen, do not correspond at all precisely to the Greek expressions that they do duty for in translation; 'moral virtue' may be a reasonably accurate translation for ἠθικὴ ἀρετή, but if so that is not because ἠθική means 'moral' nor because ἀρετή is synonymous with 'virtue'. The expression 'practical syllogism' is a more than usually unfortunate one to refer to the patterns of reasoning leading to action which occur frequently in Aristotle's writings. As we shall see in a moment, both the words 'practical' and 'syllogism' carry overtones of conflicting Aristotelian technicalities: but in addition to this the expression is not even a translation or transliteration of any expression Aristotle ever uses.

It is in the common book B of the *Ethics* at 1144a29–b1 that Aristotle comes as near as he ever comes to making 'practical syllogism' a technical term.[1] This passage is translated by Ross as follows: '. . . the syllogisms which deal with acts to be done (συλλογισμοὶ τῶν πρακτῶν) are things which involve a starting-point (ἀρχὴν ἔχοντές εἰσιν), *viz.* "since the end, i.e. what is best, is of such and such a nature" . . .' The Greek words corresponding to 'syllogisms which deal with acts to be done' (συλλογισμοὶ τῶν πρακτῶν) are taken as the Aristotelian authority for the use of the expression 'practical syllogism' by his commentators. But in fact to take συλλογισμοὶ τῶν πρακτῶν as a unit of expression is to misread the Greek, as is shown by the oddness of the participial construction ἔχοντές εἰσιν and the absence of the article after συλλογισμοί. The true sense is rather: 'Those syllogisms which contain the starting points of

[1] So Hardie, 1968, 523, whose comments on this passage I follow.

acts to be done run "since the end, or the highest good, is such and such".[1]

The passage is undoubtedly important for the understanding of Aristotle's theory of practical inference, but it concerns only a small class of what commentators call 'practical syllogisms'. It is concerned with reasonings which contain explicit mention of the highest good. Most of the practical syllogisms to be found in Aristotle do not do this: they appear to be syllogisms which a doctor or trainer might use in the endeavour to induce health and strength. Few of them explicitly mention the goal of health and strength: still less do they refer to the highest good of happiness to which healing and health may be subordinate.

'Practical syllogisms' are not, and most of them do not even look like, syllogisms. A syllogism should consist of two premises and a conclusion, all three grammatically of subject-predicate form; it should contain three terms, one of which ('the minor') occurs in subject-place in the conclusion, one of which ('the major') occures in predicate place in the conclusion, and the third of which ('the middle') occurs in both premises but not the conclusion. The premise in which the minor term occurs may be called the minor premise, and the premise in which the major term occurs may be called the major premise. A traditional syllogism of this kind is something very unlike the patterns of non-theoretical reasoning in Aristotle.

In Aristotle's writings we find practical inferences involving two, three and four premises; the conclusion is never a straightforward subject-predicate sentence; the premises are often of conditional form so that the whole looks more like an exercise in propositional calculus than in syllogistic.[2] To be sure, συλλογισμός in Greek is less technical and broader in sense than 'syllogism' in English; and even in English we can talk of hypothetical and mixed syllogisms. The point is that one must realise that a 'practical syllogism' is something even in appearance very different from a syllogism in Barbara or an inference of the form 'All xs are ys; a is an x; therefore a is a y'.

[1] Cf. Ostwald, 1962, 170; Gauthier & Jolif translate like Ross, as does Dirlmeier.

[2] For examples of inferences with many premises, and with hypothetical premises, see below, pp. 136 and 140.

The word 'practical' is as misleading as the word 'syllogism'. In several places Aristotle makes a distinction between actions that have an end separate from the activity itself and actions that have no such separate ends, or are ends in themselves (e.g. *AE* B.3, 1140a1ff; *EE* II.1, 1219a14ff; *NE* 1, 1094a5ff); the former type of activity he calls in *AE* B production, or ποίησις, and the latter conduct, or πρᾶξις. In terms of this distinction Aristotelian inferences concerning the healing of patients by doctors would not be practical inferences in the sense of being inferences leading to πρᾶξις: they are designed to lead to the production of health, and that is a ποίησις since health is distinct from healing.

What are we to call such inferences if not 'practical'? In English we can hardly call the doctors' reasonings 'poetical syllogisms', but an appropriate expression would be 'technical syllogisms' since inferences designed to produce health are an expression of the art, or τέχνη, of medicine (cf. *NE* 1.1, 1094a8). Most of Aristotle's examples of practical reasoning are in fact technical syllogisms, not syllogisms concerned with πρᾶξις in the strict sense.[1]

In spite of its misleading overtones the expression 'practical syllogism' is now so enshrined in the tradition of Aristotelian commentary that it would be foolish to attempt to substitute a new technical term.[2] I shall continue to use the expression in the broad sense in which it is customarily used. Within the broad class of practical syllogisms, then, there will be technical syllogisms concerned with production, and also syllogisms con-

[1] Aristotle is not, in fact, consistent in observing his own distinction between ποίησις and πρᾶξις. (cf. Ando, 1958, 178ff; Hintikka, 1973, 58ff.)

[2] Since 'practical syllogism' is not an Aristotelian term, an Aristotelian scholar is free to use the expression as he wishes, and so one cannot perhaps object to the attempt of Cooper (1975, 24–58) to restrict its reference to an alleged executive link between the *conclusion* of a deliberation and action. But there does seem something perverse in making such a sharp distinction between 'the practical syllogism' and 'deliberation' when the only two passages in which Aristotle applies the term 'syllogism' to reasonings about action in the *Ethics* are passages where he is explicitly talking about ethical deliberation. The greater part of Cooper's argument is devoted not to producing evidence from Aristotle for the existence of the special executive practical syllogism, but to explaining away passages where he seems clearly to be linking syllogistic and deliberation.

cerned specifically with conduct. These latter syllogisms are designed to lead to action expressive of a certain state of character (ἠθικὴ ἕξις) just as technical syllogisms lead to action expressive of skill, or τέχνη. Since 'hectic syllogism' is as impossible as 'poetic syllogism', I shall call syllogisms concerned with πρᾶξις 'ethical syllogisms'.

Though Aristotle does not use any Greek expression matching 'practical syllogism' he does have a technical expression which is closely related in sense to the English expression. This is λόγος ἕνεκα τίνος, which means literally 'a for-the-sake-of-what account', i.e. the account one would give of what one was doing if one was asked for the sake of what one was doing it. The λόγος ἕνεκα τίνος is the λόγος one would give in answer to the question ἕνεκα τίνος, just as the λόγος τί ἐστι is the λόγος one would give in answer to the question τί ἐστι, 'What is that?'. The natural way of putting the question ἕνεκα τίνος in English is 'Why are you doing that?'; but as we cannot simply call such questions 'why' questions since in English 'why' can also seek for a causal explanation, corresponding to the Greek διὰ τί, I adopt an archaic usage, calling such questions 'wherefore' questions and translating τὸ οὗ ἕνεκα as 'the wherefore'.

Let us suppose that we see an Aristotelian doctor rubbing a patient: we may ask him, 'Wherefore are you rubbing the patient?' If he replies, 'Unless he is rubbed he won't be heated', we may persist, 'Why do you want to heat him?', and he may reply, 'Unless he is heated he won't be cured.' If we know that the man is a doctor, we should now desist from our inquiries; because to the question 'Why do you want to cure him?' the answer could only be 'Because I am a doctor'. Here the pursuit of the 'wherefore' question leads to the specification of a goal which is the end of a τέχνη, namely health; so that we might be said to have uncovered a technical syllogism.

The series of question and answers, however, began with the action and worked through to the goal; whereas Aristotle insists that in practical reasoning the goal is the starting point and the action is the last thing to be discovered.[1] So the doctor's deliberation moves in the opposite direction from the dialogue we

[1] *NE* 3.3, 1112b15–19; *EE* 11.11, 1227b19–22, a passage ending τῆς μὲν οὖν νοήσεως ἀρχὴ τὸ τέλος, τῆς δὲ πράξεως ἡ τῆς νοήσεως τελευτή.

imagined. But in an artificially simple case, such as this, in which we suppose that there is one and only one action possible to achieve the goal aimed at, the same set of sentences can be used to express the answer to the question 'wherefore?' and also to express the search for the appropriate action, i.e. the deliberation. The doctor could say

> This man is to be cured
> Unless he is heated he will not be cured
> Unless he is rubbed he will not be heated

and then go on, in the one case, to the conclusion 'So that's why I am rubbing him', thus completing the answer to the 'wherefore' question, and, in the other case, to the conclusion 'So I'll rub him', which is the decision to act. But in cases where there are several ways of achieving the end, or no way to achieving it, there will not be the same isomorphism between a λόγος ἔνεκα τίνος and a piece of deliberation.

Aristotle described the possibility of such cases in his account of deliberation in *NE* 3.3:

> A doctor does not deliberate whether he shall heal, nor an orator whether he shall produce conviction, nor a statesman whether he shall establish law and order, nor does anyone else deliberate about his end. We take the end for granted and then consider in what manner and by what means it can be attained; and if it appears attainable by more than one means we look for the easiest and best; if it can be attained by one means only we consider in what manner it can be attained by that means, and how that means can be realised in its turn. We continue that process until we come to the first cause, which in order of discovery is last.

In a case where various means were possible, the formal setting out of the deliberation would clearly call for a much more complicated pattern than the simple one illustrated in the previous paragraph. One could wish that Aristotle had given us a clue how to set out the procedure for discovering the easiest and best method of curing a patient. For the comparison between various means on a scale of goodness seems to call for a type of logic quite different from the means-end reasoning which Aristotle standardly offers as an illustration of the deliberative process.

The practical reasoning involved in the discovery of the appropriate means to an end might include the exploration of a number of dead ends, as Aristotle points out in the passage quoted above:

> If we come to an impossibility, we desist; e.g. if money is needed and there is none to be had; but if a thing appears possible, we set about doing it. (1112b24–6)

It may be that when Aristotle says 'we desist' he means 'we give up the search' or 'we abandon the investigation', as Ross and Ostwald think; but there is no reason why he should mean more than that we abandon that particular avenue of research and turn to another one.

Thus, let us suppose that our Aristotelian physician begins his reasoning in a situation not where rubbing is the only means of restoring heat and health, but where the same effect might be achieved by the use of an expensive drug. The reasoning or inquiry might then proceed thus:

(1) This patient is to be cured
(2) Unless he is heated he won't be cured
(3) If he is treated with drug X or rubbed he will be heated
(4) Unless we pay much money he will not be treated with drug X
(5) We cannot pay much money
(6) So we'll rub him.

In such a case, a physician giving an answer to the 'wherefore' question asked about his rubbing would not need to give an account of his exploration of the dead-end about the drug; lines (3), (4) and (5) would then be replaced simply by 'If we rub him, he will be heated'. This will now resemble our earlier syllogism, though with the significant difference that 'unless . . . not' has been weakened to 'if'. In the present case, then, the λόγος ἕνεκα τίνος will be shorter than the syllogism expressing the deliberation.

If every line of action explored in deliberation leads to a dead

end, there will of course be no action. In such case there will
be no 'wherefore' question to be asked; no action to provide a
λόγος ἔνεκα τίνος for. Nor will there be such a λόγος for the inaction; because though there is a reason for the inaction, the
reason is the impossibility of appropriate action, and not some
good to be procured by it. It is in such a case that the difference is most marked between a λόγος ἔνεκα τίνος and a piece of
deliberation.

Both the explanation of action by a λόγος ἔνεκα τίνος and the
deliberation which is the search for the appropriate action can
be regarded as forms of practical reasoning. There are differences, as we have just seen, between the form of practical reasoning in deliberation and in explanation. But the differences
should not be exaggerated. They are exaggerated, it seems to
me, in the influential article on the practical syllogism by Professor D. J. Allan (1955). Allan argues that in the *NE* no
distinction is made between practical and theoretical reasoning
until book 6; deliberation, as described in the early books,
though preceded and followed by forms of desire, is itself intellectual and is not a distinctive operation of the practical reason.
According to Allan:

> [Aristotle's] *first* position in the *Ethics* is that all virtuous action
> involves choice, that all choice follows upon deliberation, and
> that all deliberation is concerned with the selection of means.
> As the treatise proceeds, he seems to become increasingly
> aware that in the sphere of conduct 'means' and 'end' are
> not separable in this mechanical fashion. He therefore sub-
> sequently widens his view of the procedure of choice, and
> from book vi onwards introduces the practical syllogism,
> which comprehends deliberate choice in . . . two distinct
> forms . . . performance of the act (a) as an instance of a rule
> and (b) as a step towards an end. The *second* of these cor-
> responds to deliberate action as characterized in *EN* book
> iii. The analysis of 'deliberation' itself is unaffected by this
> change, for the practical syllogism brings with it no new
> account of that process. It is the connection between 'choice'
> and 'deliberation' that is loosened from the sixth book
> onwards. (p. 338)

Allan goes on to attack 'the erroneous view that the syllogism is meant to be a kind of reasoning which precedes action and informs us what we have to do'.[1]

Allan's separation of practical reasoning from deliberation does not seem tenable either as an account of the practical syllogism in *AE* B and C, or as an account of relationship between the *AE* theory and that of the *NE*, the *EE* and the rest of the Aristotelian corpus. In the first place, the passage from the *De Anima* (III.11, 436a6ff) which he uses to introduce his own account of the practical syllogism is a passage which is explicitly concerned with the deliberative imagination (βουλευτικὴ φαντασία, 434a6). Secondly, in one of the only two places in the *AE* where συλλογισμός is explicitly used of practical reasoning, the topic is εὐβουλία, the virtue of right deliberation in pursuit of the ends determined by wisdom (B.9, 1142b23). Thirdly, though the distinction between practical and theoretical reason is not made explicit in the *NE*,[2] the practical reason introduced in the *AE* is precisely the faculty which is responsible for the ὀρθὸς λόγος or correct reasoning (*AE* B.1, 1138b25; 1139a24–b5) which in both the *NE* (2, 1103b32) and in the *EE* (1222b8) has been designated as needed for a virtuous action. And finally, in book B itself deliberation is given as the function of the practical reason (B.1, 1139a12). This is, of course, no more than we would expect, since all the deliberation described in the *NE* and *EE* has action as its purpose and upshot (e.g. *NE* 3.3, 1112a34).

Allan distinguishes two forms of practical syllogism, one involving deliberation and concerned with steps towards an end, and the other concerned with action in accordance with a rule, where no deliberation is necessary. He introduces his distinction by reference to a passage in the *De Motu Animalium* (7, 701a24) where, after various examples of practical inferences, Aristotle concludes:

---

[1] Allan's exposition is couched in terms which assume that the disputed books are at home in the *NE*; but his point, if a valid one, would apply with little modification even if the *AE* rightly belongs with the *EE*; for as we have seen there is very little difference between the accounts of deliberation in the *NE* and *EE*. But see the next note.

[2] The *EE* does seem to introduce a special part of the soul for practical

Now that the action is the conclusion is clear. But the premises of action are of two kinds, of the good and of the possible.[1]

Allan comments: 'A premise "of the possible" starts from the desirability of some End, and leads to the performance of an action as a means, whereas a premise "of the good" starts rather from the notion of a general rule to be realised in a series of actions.' Such a distinction, he thinks, would have been helpful to Aristotle in the *Ethics* (1955, 331).

Allan's comment suggests that he confused a distinction between two kinds of *premises* with a distinction between two kinds of *syllogism*. It is, I shall maintain, Aristotle's view that every practical reasoning must contain, at least tacitly, premises of both kinds. Among the examples given in the *De Motu* are the following:

One thinks that all men are to march and that one is a man oneself; straightway one marches.
If there is to be a cloak, B must be done first;
if B, then A; so one does A right away. (701a14–23)

Allan thinks that these examples illustrate two forms of reasoning, 'All men are to march' being a premise of the good, expressing a rule, 'If there is to be a cloak, B must be done first' being a premise of the possible, setting out a means-end relationship (1955, 336). But in fact all the genuinely practical premises in the examples in the *De Motu* are premises 'of the good', containing either imperatival endings (as in βαδιστέον, 'are to march') or the word 'good' (ἀγαθόν), or expressions of need; nowhere in the examples is there a statement of possibility.[2] Certainly, a premise setting out a desirable end would be a

reasoning: cf. ii.10, 1226b25, 1221b30 ἀλήθεια περὶ γενήσεως corresponding to the ἀλήθεια πρακτική of B.

[1] I quote Farquahrason's translation which is used by Allan. The Greek corresponding to 'premises of action' is αἱ προτάσεις αἱ ποιητικαί and the syllogism quoted in illustration is in fact a technical one.

[2] Of course statements of necessity—e.g. 'If there is to be a cloak, B must be done first' (εἰ ἱμάτιον ἔσται, ἀνάγκη τόδε πρῶτον—are tantamount to statements of impossibility—without B being done first it is impossible for

premise 'of the good', not 'of the possible' as Allan suggests. What the reference to possibility means is this: practical reasoning can only come to a successful end when it reaches some action which is in the agent's power, some state of affairs which he can bring about.[1]

In practical reasoning, after each statement (initial or subsequent) that a certain state of affairs is good, the agent must ask himself 'Is this a state of affairs I can here and now bring about?' If the answer is No, he must look for some further means to that state of affairs; if it is Yes, then we have the desired 'premise of the possible', and we can move into action. It is to be regretted that Aristotle does not set out in detail and with examples the nature of reasoning about the possible. In the *De Motu* he merely throws in as an afterthought that there also have to be premises about the possible as well as premises about the good. But that, in effect, is also what he does in the passages of the *NE* and *EE* concerned with deliberation. There is not the difference that Allan claims between the *De Motu* and the ethical works.

A piece of practical reasoning, set out in full, would have to begin with a premise of the good and end with a premise of the possible. What of the intermediate premises set out in the *De Motu* and elsewhere such as 'I am a man', 'A cloak is a covering', 'If there is to be a cloak, B must be done first'? These are not, strictly speaking, either premises of the good or premises of the possible; their function in practical reasoning is to mediate the transition from one premise of the good to another premise of the good, or from one premise of the possible to another. Any actual case of practical reasoning can be set out as a number of premises of the good plus one premise of the possible, or a number of premises of the possible plus one premise of the good.

---

there to be a cloak; but if this was what Aristotle had in mind it would have been simpler to say that practical premises come in two kinds, the good and the necessary.

[1] This is insisted on in the *NE*: 'If a thing appears possible we try to do it: by 'possible' things I mean things that might be brought about by our own efforts' 1112b26; and in the *EE*: 'We continue the deliberation until we have brought the commencement of the production to a point in our own power' 1226b13.

To illustrate this, we return to our physician. His reasoning can be set out in the two following parallel forms:

I am to heal this patient (p. of good)	I am to heal this patient (p. of good)
If he is rubbed, he will be healed (transition)	I can rub this patient (p. of possible)
I am to rub this patient (p. of good)	If he is rubbed, he will be healed (transition)
I am to rub this patient (p. of possible)	I can heal this patient (p. of possible)
So I'll rub him (conclusion)	So I'll rub him (conclusion).

In each of these formulations the reasoning continues until there is a match between a premise of the good and a premise of the possible. But one can see why Aristotle prefers the formulation in which the transitional premises link one premise of the good with another premise of the good, rather than the form in which the transitional premises link premises of the possible with each other. Because in the form in which the transitions are between premises of the good, the match takes place at the point at which immediately performable action comes into consideration. So the formulation represents the process of deliberation much more successfully than the alternative formulation does.

Allan's account of Aristotle's distinction between the two kinds of premises is criticised also by Hintikka (1973, 54) who writes:

> The distinction is certainly a distinction between the major and the minor premise and not a distinction between two different types of minor (or major) premises.

Having quoted *NE* 3, 1112b27 on the meaning of 'possible', he concludes:

> Premises concerning the possible may therefore be taken to

be concerned with what we can do in a particular situation, i.e. they are the minor premises of a practical syllogism.

Hintikka's own account of the distinction seems open to criticism. In particular his use of the expression 'minor premise', though following the practice of a number of commentators, is unhappy. First, talk of 'the major premise' and 'the minor premise' suggests that practical reasoning, like the traditional Aristotelian syllogism, involves exactly two premises, whereas Aristotle is very flexible in the number of premises he allows. Secondly, Aristotle himself never uses the expressions 'major' and 'minor' of practical premises. For that matter, in the *Prior Analytics* in which he introduces the expressions, they are used exclusively of the terms of a proposition, not of the propositions themselves. Aristotle does speak of the premises of practical reasoning as divided into universal (καθόλου) and particular (κατὰ μέρος, or καθ' ἔκαστα) in a number of passages (e.g. *AE* B.3, 1147a2, 1147a25). One of these is translated by Hintikka thus:

> In a practical syllogism the major premise is an opinion, while the minor premise deals with particular things, which are the province of perception.

But the Greek has merely:

> The one is a universal opinion, the other deals with particular things which are the province of perception. (1147a25)

The distinction between universal and particular premises is totally different from that between major and minor terms in the *Analytics* or between major and minor premises in post-Aristotelian terminology.

Some philosophers (including Hintikka) think that the conclusion of a practical syllogism is an action. It is difficult to see any way in which, on this view, the terms 'major' and 'minor' can be applied to the practical syllogism either in their Aristotelian or in their post-Aristotelian sense. For since the minor term is the subject of the conclusion-proposition, and the major term is the predicate of the conclusion-proposition, there can be neither minor nor major term, and therefore neither minor nor major premise, where there is no conclusion-proposition at all.

However, I shall argue later that it is incorrect to say that the conclusion of a practical inference *must* be an action. One might take a verbalisation of a decision to act, such as 'Now I will march' as corresponding to the conclusion of a theoretical decision. In an argument to this conclusion one might take a premise about myself as minor, and a premise about marching as major. But then two difficulties arise. First, even in the simple syllogism 'All men are to march now; I am a man; so I'll march now' a difficulty arises: we do not seem to have the same predicate in the conclusion as in the first premise, so that there is an incorrectness in calling it 'major'. Secondly, in more complicated syllogisms such as 'Dry food is good for every man; I am a man; this is chicken; chicken is dry; so I'll eat this' (cf. *AE* c, 1147a5ff) there will be premises which on this test are neither major nor minor.[1]

Aristotle does, however, use the expression 'middle term' in connection with practical reasoning. In *AE* b.9, in the discussion or εὐβουλία, or excellence in deliberation, we read:

> It is possible to attain something good by a false syllogism and to hit on what one should do but by the wrong route, when the middle term is false. This process of achieving the right goal but not by the right route is something less than excellence in deliberation. (1142b23)

An instance of such a process might be as follows. Someone, in pursuit of health, might believe falsely that heavy meats were conducive to health, and further believe falsely that chicken was heavy meat, and thus reach the conclusion that he should eat chicken. The conclusion, on Aristotelian medical theory, would be a correct one (cf. *AE* b, 1141b20), but would have been reached from false premises, the middle term 'heavy'

---

[1] The complicated, many-premise syllogisms can, sometimes if not always, be represented as sequences of syllogisms. But if we do so, then the 'major' premise which will be result will be something far removed from generalisations such as 'Dry food is good for any man' which commentators usually have in mind when they talk of major premises.

being false of chicken.[1] Since, in an ordinary syllogism, the
middle term is the term that does not appear in the conclusion,
and since in any practical reasoning at least one term will appear
which does not appear in the conclusion however the conclusion is conceived, there is not the same inappropriateness in
talking of 'the middle term' in a practical syllogism as there is in
talking of 'the major' or 'the minor'.[2]

---

[1] Commentators, both ancient and modern, assume that Aristotle has
in mind the achieving of desirable goals by ethically undesirable means,
e.g. freeing oneself from prison by committing adultery with the gaoler's
wife. But in the first place in the present passage Aristotle is making a general
point about deliberation: the restriction of εὐβουλία to the goals of φρόνησις
rather than those of τέχνη is not made until six lines later at 1142b30; and
secondly it is hard to see how there is anything *false* in the premise 'Committing adultery with the gaoler's wife is a way of getting out of prison'
simply on the grounds that committing adultery is wrong.

Aristotle himself offers an illustration of the use of 'middle' in a piece of
practical reasoning concerned with the beneficial effects of a post-prandial
stroll in *Post. An.* 94b8–26. As no commentator has produced a syllogism
which is both valid and in accord with Aristotle's instructions here I pass
over the passage in silence.

[2] The only inappropriateness is in speaking of '*the* middle' in a case where
many terms appear in the premises which do not appear in the conclusion.

11. *Technical Reasoning I: The Initial Premise*

If we wish to understand Aristotle's theory of practical reasoning, then, rather than start from analogies with theoretical syllogisms, it is better to try to isolate the elements which occur in the various examples and see how best they can be classified on their own merits. Since the majority of Aristotle's illustrations appear to concern technical reasonings rather than ethical ones, I shall begin by trying to set out the structure of a technical syllogism, and then turn to the extensions or modifications which are necessary in the case of ethical syllogisms.

Technical reasoning, for Aristotle, must pass through at least three steps; and however many steps it passes through they can be grouped into three stages, initial, intermediate, and ultimate. The initial stage of technical reasoning is concerned with the end which the τέχνη in question pursues—health in the case of medicine, victory in the case of strategy and so on. The intermediate stage is concerned with the discovery and evaluation of means. The ultimate stage is concerned with decision and action.[1]

The first or initial stage is concerned with an end or goal: this we are told by Aristotle many times in different contexts. Consider for instance the following passages from the accounts of deliberation in the *NE* and *EE*:

> We deliberate not about ends but about means. For a doctor does not deliberate whether he should heal, nor an orator whether he shall carry conviction . . . They assume the end (*NE* 3.3, 1112b11–15). Nobody deliberates about his end; this is a starting point (ἀρχή) and postulate (ὑπόθεσις) like the postulates in theoretical science. (*EE* ii.10, 1227a9–10)[2]

[1] I have chosen the terms to correspond to Aristotle's ἀρχή, μεταξύ, and ἔσχατον.

[2] See also several other passages in the *EE*: 1226b10, 1227a16, 1227b25.

From these and other passages it is clear that the goal or end is mentioned at the beginning of a piece of technical reasoning. But in what form will the mention of the goal appear? There are a number of possibilities, several of which are given plausibility by different passages in Aristotle:

(1) I want to heal
(2) Health is good
(3) I shall heal
(4) This patient is to be healed
(5) Health is of such-and-such a nature.

Let us consider these different proposed formulations in turn.

(1) *I want to heal*. Aristotle often says that the end is an object of wanting or volition, and he connects this with his claim that the end is the beginning of the deliberation which leads to purposive choice. (Thus, e.g., at *NE* 3.2: 'Volition relates rather to the end, choice to the means; for instance we will to be healthy, but we choose the acts which will make us healthy.') Moreover, it seems in general true that practical reasoning about how to produce a certain state of affairs will only lead to action if that state of affairs is itself wanted. Hence, one might think that the starting premise of a piece of practical inference ought to be the report of a desire.

Professor Anscombe (1963, 66) has argued strongly that it is a mistake to put 'I want' into a premise if we are to give a formal account of practical reasoning. She observes that 'I want this, so I'll do it' is not a piece of practical reasoning, because no calculation is involved. Aristotle would agree. He gives as an example of an action performed without reasoning the case in which desire says 'I must drink', a drink is in sight, and drinking immediately follows (*De Motu* 7, 701a32). From this passage it is clear that he does not think that the fact that an action is in fulfilment of an expressed appetite (ἐπιθυμία) is enough to make it the upshot of practical reasoning; and it is further significant that the expression of the desire is not itself a report of a desire; there is no premise 'I want a drink'. But because not every expression of desire is a fit initial premise of practical reasoning it does not of course follow that no fit initial premise of practical reasoning is a desire or volition. Anscombe's reasons for this further conclusion were not wholly clear in *Intention*, and some of her readers were unconvinced (e.g. Gauthier, 1963, 28–30).

In a more recent study (1974, IV.3) Anscombe offers a demonstration that wanting or intending should not be put into a formulation of a practical inference. Just as one can draw conclusions from theoretical premises which one does not believe, so, she argues, one can draw practical conclusions from practical premises without sharing the objectives that they express. Thus a slave may act in accordance with his master's aims, perhaps even without believing the factual premises involved, much less sharing the aims:

> Not aiming at what the directing will aims at, not believing his premises, but still drawing the conclusion in action . . . corresponds to not believing the assertions and not believing the conclusion but still drawing the conclusion in the theoretical case.

Thus, it is as incorrect to put wanting into the premise of a practical inference as it would be to represent theoretical inference in terms of belief.

The parallel is broadly convincing, but it needs to be drawn out and modified. If drawing a practical conclusion means acting, or deciding to act, then its theoretical parallel is belief in the conclusion of an argument; the parallel to theoretically drawing a conclusion, in the sense of agreeing that if the premises are true then the conclusion is true, is something different, namely, agreeing that if the premises express a good to be realised, then the conclusion expresses a good thing to do. But an agent is only acting on those premises if he accepts them as in some way expressing *his good*. If a slave reasons from his master's orders to an obedient action, the master's aim expressed in his orders is not the starting point of the slave's practical reasoning; the slave's aim, as Anscombe realises, is likely to be the avoidance of trouble; for him the existence of the order is a secondary, intermediate, premise.

Though no one could act on a piece of practical reasoning

unless he wanted the good specified in the initial premise, there can surely be practical reasoning from premises concerning states of affairs which the reasoner does not want. A cynical public relations officer may devise means of promoting causes he does not believe in, an architect may draw plans to specifications he considers ludicrous, and a historian may consider whether the policies of a long-dead ruler were reasonable, given his objectives and beliefs, and, if not, what they should have been instead. These reasonings have a claim to be called practical even when they are not, and in the historical case could not be, put into effect in action. The mark of practical reasoning as opposed to theoretical reasoning is not that it culminates in action, but that in the same sense in which theoretical reasoning seeks to pass from the true to the true, practical reasoning seeks to pass from the good to the good. One can draw practical conclusions from bad objectives as one can draw theoretical conclusions from false premises; but even in such cases one is passing from hypothetical good to hypothetical good, just as in the theoretical cases one is passing from hypothetical truth to hypothetical truth.[1]

We may agree that it is a mistake to include a report of a psychological pro-attitude among the premises of a piece of practical reasoning. It will, however, be apt to include such a report when *explaining* an action as performed on the basis of a piece of practical reasoning. These conclusions accord well with Aristotle's practice; for when giving examples of practical reasoning he does not include statements of wants in the premises, while he often insists on the role that desire of the end plays in the causation of action.

(2) *Health is good.* In support of the suggestion that the initial premise of a practical syllogism is of the form 'X is good' one might quote the example in the *De Motu* 'I should make some-

---

[1] Anscombe writes: 'There would be no point in (theoretical) proof patterns if they were never to be plugged into believing minds, if nothing were ever asserted; and equally no point in patterns of practical reasoning if nothing were aimed at.' The parallel would, I think, have been more exact and more revealing had the remark concluded: '. . . and equally no point in patterns of practical inference if they were never to be plugged into desiring wills, if nothing were ever decided upon.'

thing good, a house is a good' which is said to lead to the immediate making of a house (*DMA* 701a17). This rather odd syllogism is not in fact a technical syllogism, for it does not *begin* with the end or goal of an art; for a house is the goal of housebuilding as health is the goal of medicine, and this is not mentioned until the second premise.

Very similar to 'X is good' as an initial premise would be a premise of the form 'X is the end'; and in support of the idea that this is the correct formulation one might appeal to the passages already quoted from the *EE* and *NE* discussions of delineration. If the end, say health, is 'assumed' or is a 'postulate', does that not mean that there is assumed or postulated a proposition to the effect that health is the end? One might seek to support this by quoting the parallel with theoretical postulates: we take the end as our starting point, we are told,

> just as in geometry we argue that if the angles of the triangle are equal to two right angles, then so and so must be the case. (EE II. 11, 1227b32; cf. II.6, 1222b33)

But in fact the parallel tells the other way. The theoretical postulate is not a postulate *that* something is a first principle, but the postulation *of* something which is then used as a first principle, an axiom from which conclusions are deduced. Similarly, a technical postulate should not be the postulation *that* something is an end, but the postulation of a proposition concerning the nature of that which is postulated as an end.

(3) *I shall heal.* One might argue that the end appears in the initial premise in the form of a decision to realise it. The argument would be very simple. *NE* 3.3 tells us that the doctor does not deliberate about whether he should heal, but assumes the end. What he assumes, surely, is what he does not deliberate about: and this is precisely the proposition 'I shall heal'.

The difficulty here is in deciding how to interpret 'He should heal'. If interpreted as referring to a decision expressible as 'I shall heal', then this cannot be Aristotle's understanding of the initial premise of a practical syllogism: for the nearest Aristotelian concept to our concept of decision is προαίρεσις, and a προαίρεσις is the upshot, not the beginning, of a piece of practical reasoning. We can take the initial premise of the reasoning as 'I should heal' or 'I am to heal', however, where this expresses not a decision—nor yet, at the other extreme, a duty—but a pro-attitude or ὄρεξις towards the goal of the health.[1] So understood, the initial premise 'I am to heal' is for logical purposes equivalent in the circumstances of technical deliberation to the premise 'This patient is to be healed', which was the fourth proposed interpretation, to which we now turn.

(4) *This patient is to be healed.* 'The doctor does not inquire whether one ought to be healthy or not, but whether one ought to walk or not,' says the *EE* (II.8, 1227b25). Again, we may reason that what he assumes is what he does not inquire about, *viz.* that his patient is to be made healthy.[2]

It has often been suggested that the essential characteristic of the initial premise of a practical syllogism is its prescriptive nature (e.g. Anscombe, 1973, 65).[3] The occurrence of δεῖ ('should' or 'is to') or of gerundive forms does not necessarily, as Anscombe insists, give it an ethical content or make it into a moral judgment. Nor, I should maintain, does the occurrence

[1] The *expression* of a pro-attitude is of course quite different from the *report* of a pro-attitude, which is what was ruled out in the consideration of the first alternative above.

[2] Rackham makes Aristotle give 'So-and-so is to be healthy' explicitly as the initial premise of the practical syllogism, by emending the δεῖ τόδε ὑγιαίνειν of the MSS to δεῖ τόνδε ὑγιαίνειν, at 1227b31. But I shall shortly propose a more appropriate emendation to the passage.

[3] Thus, for instance, J. P. Hierro (1970, 171) collects six examples of practical syllogisms from various works of Aristotle and says: 'En los primeros cinco ejemplos la primera premise es un juicio normativo, no esta claro de que tipo y, desde luego, no necessariamente de tipo moral. Los terminos utilizados son: βαδιστέον en los dos primeros ejemplos; ποιητέον en los dos siguientes, y δεῖ en el quinto.' He then considers the dry food syllogism of *AE* c.3, 1147a1ff and concludes that, containing as it does the word συμφέρει it is an evaluative rather than a normative judgment: 'Peros notese que tambien esta premisa es, como las anteriores, prescriptiva, puesto que ultizamos este ultimo termino come genero de los juicios normativos, valorativos e imperativos.' I think that the contrast Hierro draws between normative and evaluative judgments is foreign to Aristotle in this context; and certainly, for reasons shortly to be given, it is incorrect to take δεῖ as a mark of the normative in contrast to συμφέρει as a mark of the evaluative.

of δεῖ in a premise necessarily fit it to be an initial premise, whether of technical or ethical reasoning.

In the *Topics* it appears as a commonplace that τὸ δέον can be divided into sub-classes of τὸ σύμφερον and τὸ καλόν (2.3, 110b10). Given this, we may conclude that there may be no difference between saying that every man should (δεῖ) eat dry food, and saying that dry food suits (συμφέρει) every man; whether the syllogism is ethical or technical will depend on what is the end to which dry food συμφέρει, on what is the benefit which dry food confers. Presumably, in the case in point when Aristotle uses this example in *AE* c (1147a1ff) the end in question is health, so that his syllogism is a technical one, and the premise is tantamount to: dry food is conducive to health. But if that is so then a premise such as the one about dry food— whether couched in the δεῖ form or the συμφέρει form—is not a genuine initial premise; for it does not concern the end, and we know that the initial premise is about the end.[1]

A premise such as 'This man is to be healed', however, *is* a prescriptive premise about the end, and so is suitable to be an initial premise. But it is clear from what Aristotle says in several places that it needs completing with an enunciation of the nature of the end if it is to be an expression of the basis of practical reasoning.

(5) *Health is of such-and-such a nature.* It is in the *Metaphysics* that Aristotle states most explicitly that an account of the nature of the end stands at the commencement of a piece of practical reasoning:

A healthy patient is produced as a result of the following reasoning: since health is so-and-so, if the patient is to be healthy, he must have such-and-such a quality ... (*Met.* Z.7, 1032b8)

---

[1] One can speak also of things which are συμφέροντα to the good of man as such, the end which is the special object of prudence (*AE* b.9, 1142b32); these can be called τὰ συμφέροντα *par excellence* (*NE* 3.1, 1110b31). To say that something is σύμφερον in the sense is not incompatible with saying that it is καλόν. This is a point to which we must return when we turn from the technical to the ethical syllogism.

The starting point of the healing is 'the definition and know-ledge' of health in the doctor's mind.

The *Metaphysics* teaching is clearly enunciated also in the *EE* if not in the *NE*. The 'definition and knowledge' which is in the doctor's mind might be called a *theory* of health, since it is what teachers of medicine pass on to their pupils. This is made clear in *EE* 1.8 (1218b20):

> That the end stands in a causal relation to the means subordinate to it is shown by the method of teachers; they prove that the means are severally good by giving a definition of the end, because the end aimed at is a cause: for instance, since to be healthy is so-and-so, necessarily what conduces to health must be so-and-so.

Again, in a passage already considered:

> As in the theoretical disciplines it is postulates which are the starting points, so in productive disciplines it is the end which is the starting point and postulate; since, if this is what being healthy is, if that is to come about then such and such must be provided[1]—just as in the other case, if the angles of a triangle equal two right angles, such and such necessarily follows. (*EE* II.11, 1227b32)

Putting together, therefore, what Aristotle tells us about the initial premise or starting point of practical reasoning, we can say that it consists of a statement of the end to be pursued plus a definition, account, or theory of the nature of that end. In a case of technical reasoning designed to produce health, for instance, it will be of the form 'So-and-so is to be made healthy, and being healthy is such-and-such'. All this can reasonably be summed up in the phrase traditional among commentators that the initial premise of a piece of practical reasoning is 'the specification of an end'.

---

[1] Reading ἐπειδὴ εἰ τόδε ὑγιαίνειν, ἀνάγκη ὑπάρξαι εἰ ἔσται ἐκεῖνο. The MSS read δεῖ τόδε for εἰ τόδε; the emendation I propose is as simple as Rackham's δεῖ τόνδε or Susemihl's δεῖ τόδε but gives a better sense: it is sup-ported by the parallels quoted above and by the fact that on Rackham's or Susemihl's readings the ἐπειδή clause is a duplicate of the εἰ clause and the overall construction is unclear.

12. *Technical Reasoning II: From Premises to Conclusion*

We may turn from the initial premise to the other premises of practical reasoning. These can be grouped into two kinds, intermediate and ultimate premises.

Intermediate premises are often expressed as conditionals. The conditional sentences which appear in the fragments of technical syllogisms given by Aristotle—e.g. 'If the patient is to be healthy his humours must be balanced, If his humours are to be balanced he must be heated'—are not so much independent premises as conclusions from the first premise in its capacity as a theory of the good sought by the art in question (in this case health). We can, I have suggested, treat these premises as being, or providing links between, 'premises of the good': the conditionals as it were transmit the goodness of the end (which occurs in the protasis of the first conditional) to the means (which are mentioned in the apodoses of the conditionals). Something which is wholesome, i.e. a means to health, will be an efficient cause for the existence of health; but it is not the cause of the goodness of health; on the contrary it is the goodness of health which is the cause of the goodness of the means to health (cf. *EE* 1.8, 1218b22).

In the case of deliberation, the conditional premises will occur in answer to the question 'By what means?' (διὰ τίνων;) (*NE* 3, 1112b16–18). They are premises of the same kind as those introduced by συμφέρει: it is all one whether one says, in the course of practical reasoning,

If he eats dry food, he will be healthy

or

Dry food is conducive to his health.

For this reason even a universal such as 'Dry food suits any man' should be treated as an intermediate, and not as an initial, premise: in a fully spelt out piece of technical reasoning it would appear subordinate to an original premise which contained a theory of human health: 'Since human health is such and such, dry food is conducive to any man's health . . .'

In Aristotle's examples there are other premises which come between the specification of the goal and the drawing of the conclusion which are premises of quite a different kind. For instance 'This (bit of food) is of such and such a kind' (*AE* c.3, 1147a7), 'This is sweet' (1147a29). These are sense-judgments made about individuals (cf. *AE* b.11, 1143b5; c.3, 1147b10). Other, comparable, premises concern the agent's ability to perform some action without further deliberation. The physician continues to reason, Aristotle says, until he arrives at some ultimate (ἔσχατον) which he can himself produce (*Met. Z*.7, 1032b10). We continue the process of deliberation until we come to the first link in the chain of causation, which is the ultimate step in the order of discovery (*NE* 3.3, 112b19). The end-point of reasoning is the starting point of action (*EE* ii.11, 1227b34). These premises involving sense-perception and immediate awareness of one's ability we may call 'ultimate' premises since they contain, if fully spelt out, a term such as a demonstrative which Aristotle would call an 'ultimate' (ἔσχατον).[1]

In *Metaphysics Δ*, when setting out the meanings of 'cause'

---

[1] Cooper (1975, 183–6) devotes an appendix to the meaning of ἔσχατον in Aristotle. ' "Last",' he says, in the passages in the *AE*, 'means "last in the order of deliberation" and', he goes on to claim, 'it does not refer to individuals, but to specific kinds of things.' I agree that ἔσχατον does not *mean* individual, but I am unconvinced by Cooper's claim that Aristotle is not using it in these passages to refer to individuals. Of course Cooper is right that actions decided on after deliberation are actions of a specific kind: that is because actions are only individuated by being performed, so that a decision *can* only be to perform an action answering to a certain description (e.g. to the description 'act of eating some of this chicken'). But it seems clear that Aristotle's examples are meant to illustrate deliberations leading up to eating some of *this* chicken *now*. They are not deliberations about the goodness of chicken completely in the air, carried out at leisure and to be put away into cold storage on the off chance that I may one day encounter some chicken, which is what they seem to be on Cooper's account (p.38).

Aristotle lists his Four Causes and then lists means to an end as a fifth sort. Among the things we call causes, he says (2, 1013b1ff), there is

> also, anything that comes to be as a means to an end when what effected the change was something else, as for instance, of health, slimming or purging, or medicines or instruments: for all these are for the sake of the end, but differ from one another in that some are instruments, others actions.

Perceptible objects mentioned in ultimate premises of a technical inference will be instruments; actions mentioned in the final premise, e.g. 'So I'll rub him', would belong to the other category of means. What matters is that in each case the ultimate premise of the practical reasoning should specify something within the agent's power: an instrument within his grasp, an action within his repertoire and so on:

> Men deliberate about the means leading to their end—is this conducive to it, or this; and if this is thought to be the right thing to do, how will it be procured? This deliberation we all pursue until we have traced back the starting point of the productive process to ourselves . . . A man deliberates about those contingent means towards the end that are in our own power. (*EE* II.10, 1226b17–1227a18)

> If a thing appears possible we set about doing it. By 'possible' I mean things that can be brought about by our own agency . . . Sometimes the object of our investigation is to find the instruments we need, and sometimes to find how to use them. (*NE* 3, 1112b25–30)

Actions are more important than instruments, since every instrument is for the sake of action (*De Partibus* 645b15–17) and the use of an instrument can be regarded as a particular style of action. So the final premise in the practical inference can always be represented as concerned with an action in the agent's power: an action which may be the use of an instrument (cutting with a saw, eating a piece of bread, etc.). The function of the occurrence of a premise such as 'This is bread' (*NE* 3,

K

1113a1) or 'Here is some dry food' in a piece of practical inference is tantamount to 'Eating bread is here and now in my power', 'Taking dry food is here and now in my power'. Both formulations can be regarded as formulations of premises 'of the possible' as Aristotle put it in the *De Motu Animalium*.

I maintained in an earlier chapter that in every practical inference there must be, explicitly or implicitly, at least one premise of the good and one premise of the possible. But the majority of the premises which we are given in illustration are not obviously of either of these forms. For instance we have 'If that is to come about, this must be procured' (*EE* II, 1127b32) 'Light meats are digestible' 'Chicken is light' (*AE* B.7, 1141b19) 'Such and such a kind of food is dry' (*AE* C.3, 1147a6) 'A cloak is a covering' 'If there is to be a cloak such and such must be the case' (*De Motu* 7, 701a22). As I suggested earlier, these can be used to mediate the transition from one premise of the good to another premise of the good, or from one premise of the possible to another premise of the possible. Let us spell this out a little more fully.

Consider the reasoning suggested by *Met. Z*.7. once more:

(1) This man is to be healed
(2) Health being the kind of thing it is, humours must be balanced (1032b8, b19)
(3) If he is heated, his humours will be balanced (1032b20)
(4) If he is rubbed, he will be heated (1032b26)
(5) Rubbing is in my power (1032b21).

We take it that this line of reasoning leads up to the doctor rubbing the patient and thus, it is to be hoped, healing him. The first four steps in the argument can all be looked at as 'premises of the good', or more strictly as generating a succession of premises of the good from the initial goal premise, in the following way:

(1') Healing this man is a good thing to do
(2') So, given 2, balancing the humours of this man is a good thing to do
(3') So, given 3, heating him is a good thing to do
(4') So, given 4, rubbing him is a good thing to do
(5') Rubbing him is in my power.

But it would also be possible to look on the second, third, and fourth premises as premises 'of the possible' answering an inquiry about ways and means:

(1″) This man is to be healed
How can I heal him?
(2″) I can heal him by balancing his humours
How can I balance his humours?
(3″) I can balance his humours by heating him
How can I heat him?
(4″) I can heat him by rubbing him
Rubbing him is in my power.

It is clear that the force of the reasoning is the same in each case. It does not matter much whether we look on the factual conditionals as premises of the good or of the possible; as was said above, what matters is that at some point in the reasoning a description of what is in my power should coincide with a description of something which is a good thing to do. The second way of setting out the premises is perhaps the most natural way to give an explanation or justification of a thing done, and the third the most natural way of setting out a pattern of deliberation about a thing to do. Presumably such a pattern of deliberation is to be continued until we reach a description of an action which is in a certain sense basic: an action, such as rubbing, which can be done without being done *by* doing something else.

Besides classifying premises of practical reasoning as being 'of the good' or 'of the possible' Aristotle classes them as universal (καθόλου), particular (κατὰ μέρος) and individual (καθ᾽ ἕκαστον). How does the second classification relate to the first? A proposition about goodness could no doubt be individual: the animal ποτέον μοι (I must drink) is probably of this kind. But it is not a premise of practical *reasoning*: the mark of such reasoning is that it should include a universal judgment (καθόλου ὑπόληψις) (so *De Motu* 701a28; *AE* B.2, 1139b29; *AE* c.3, 1147b4). On the other hand, the ἔσχατον premise must be individual: it must be about what is here and now within the power of a particular agent (e.g. *AE* c, 1147a30). So that the two distinctions so far connect with each other: the initial

premise will be universal and of the good, the ultimate premise
will be individual and of the possible.

But in the case of the intermediate premises it is not always
easy to see the appropriate classification by extent. The
distinction between universal and particular premises is most
explicitly drawn in the discussion of incontinence in *AE* c.3,
1147a1ff. There we read, following Bywater's text:

> Since there are two kinds of premises, there is nothing to
> prevent a man's having both premises and acting against his
> knowledge, provided that he is using only the universal
> premise and not the particular; for it is individual acts which
> get done. And there are also two kinds of universal term: one
> is predicable of the agent, the other of the object; e.g. 'Dry
> food is good for every man' and 'I am a man' or 'Such-and-
> such food is dry'; but whether 'This good is such-and-such' is
> an item which he may fail to have, or fail to exercise.

In this passage it is natural to think that 'Dry food is good for
every man' is a universal premise, 'Such-and-such food is dry'
is a particular premise, and 'I am a man' and 'This food is
such-and-such' are individual premises. It may be that this is
the case, but it is not at all clear from the text that Aristotle
wishes to make the distinction in this way. He is not in fact
giving examples of universal and particular premises here. The
nearest examples given and expressly named are the universal
'Everything sweet is to be tasted' and the individual 'This is
sweet' a page later (1147a39). When Aristotle discusses the
premise 'Dry food is good for every man' he is giving examples
of universal terms ('dry' and 'man'), not of universal premises.
And it seems that he is not making any systematic distinction
between 'particular' and 'individual' here, but rather using the
two expressions as synonyms.[1]

To count as universal, a premise of practical reasoning, I

[1] That such is his usage in the *Ethics* is most strongly suggested by *EE*
1248b8–12. καθόλου is contrasted with κατὰ μέρος at *NE* 3, 1107a30 and
AE c, 1147a3, and with καθ' ἕκαστον at *NE* 2, 1104a5, *AE* B, 1141b15, *AE*
c, 1143b5); I do not find any passage where the two latter expressions are
contrasted with each other in the *Ethics*.

conjecture, must contain an indication of value (be a premise 'of the good') and must contain at least one universal quantifier or expression of generality. These conditions are necessary, but not, I think, sufficient: I doubt if Aristotle would have regarded 'I must mop up every last drop of this delicious gravy' as a universal practical premise in spite of containing the quantifier 'every' and the evaluative adjective 'delicious'. The type of value and universality necessary is a special one: the premise must state that a certain *kind* of thing or action is good for a certain *kind* of agent. Thus the standard form of universal premise will be: an agent of such and such a kind should do an act of such and such a kind; or: a thing of such and such a kind is good for an agent of such and such a kind. (The former is given as the pattern of καθόλου ὑπόληψις in the *De Anima*, 434a16, and the latter is illustrated by the dry food premise of *AE* c.3, 1147a3ff.) A premise containing only one quantifier (e.g. 'must taste everything sweet' in *AE* c.3, 1147a29) can be regarded as universal only if it is thought of as applying to the agent *qua* belonging to a certain class. In such a case its application to him could be derived from a generalisation which might be explicitly stated. (Thus Mrs Beeton's *Household Management* may state that the head pastrycook must taste everything sweet before it leaves the kitchen.)

Aristotle seems to insist, in the fact of his own examples, that a practical syllogism contains only *two* premises (e.g. *AE* b.11, 1143b3; *AE* c, 1147a1, a25). The only way to make his practice fit the theory in this respect seems to be to regard all the premises of the good as being conjoined to make the universal premise, and all the premises of the possible as being conjoined to make the singular premise. The intermediate premises, in the light of what was said above, can be included in either conjunction at choice. Thus the dry food syllogism could be treated either thus:

Universal: Dry food suits any man, and chicken is dry
Particular: I am a man and here is some chicken

or thus:

Universal: Dry food suits any man

Particular: I am a man and chicken is dry and here is some chicken.[1]

The most favoured alternative among commentators who wish to fit Aristotle's examples into a two-premise pattern is to treat them as so many sorites. Thus, we would get

> Dry food suits any man
> I am a man
> Dry food suits me

as the first syllogism of the chain, followed by:

> Dry food suits me
> Chicken is dry food
> Chicken suits me

as the second, with the sorites being formed by dropping the conclusion of each of these syllogisms and prefacing their premises, one after the other, to the final syllogism of the chain:

> Chicken suits me
> This is chicken
> This suits me.

One can well understand why someone might want to abbreviate this tedious reasoning into something more like the text of *AE* c.3; and one might support this reading of the dry food syllogism by appeal to an example offered in the *De Motu Animalium*:

> I need a covering
> A cloak is a covering
> I need a cloak
> I should make what I need
> I need a cloak
> I should make a cloak. (701a8–10)

If we read the *Ethics* passage in this way we do not solve the problem but only change it: for in every passage where Aristotle talks as if there was a *pair* of premises he also talks as if there

---

[1] I have argued elsewhere (Kenny, 1966, 172) that in the relevant passage Aristotle does in fact treat it in the second way. See below, pp. 155ff.

was *one* pair of premises. Only the major of the first syllogism and the minor of the last syllogism of the sorites fit what we know from elsewhere about practical premises. It is as easy to rewrite the *De Motu* example to match the *Ethics* one as *vice versa*—thus:

> Universal: Every man should make what he needs
> Particular: I am a man, and I need a covering, and a cloak is a covering.

It is indeed only by supplying some such Tolstoyan general premise that one can make the *De Motu* example a plausible practical syllogism.

If we allow practical premises to be composite, then it will be possible to separate out, in the initial premise, the universal and the evaluative element. This was indeed the conclusion to which we were forced in considering the nature of the initial premise of technical reason: our discussion suggested that the premise should take some form as this:

> This man is to be healthy, and health is balancing the humours.

The second premise, correspondingly, will be a composite such as

> Here is drug X, and drug X will balance his humours.

Or, in the more explicit conditional Aristotle prefers sometimes:

> I can give him drug X and if I give him drug X I will balance his humours.[1]

Thus if we ask how we are to classify the premises given by Aristotle which are neither universal value judgments nor propositions about individuals, the answer is that they are to appear in conjuncts in complex propositions which as a whole contain universal value judgments or individual sense-judgments. This will enable us to accept Aristotle's view that there

---

[1] It may be that Aristotle would have regarded the universal premise of the art of medicine as being purely general, as 'Every man ought to be healthy, and such and such is what health is'. In which case 'This man ought to be healthy' would be derived from the general premise.

are only *two* premises. But in practice it is easier—as Aristotle's own practice shows—to treat the conjoined items as separate atomic premises.

What is the conclusion of a piece of practical reasoning? If we are to be guided by the discussions of deliberation in the *NE, EE* and *AE* we must say that it is a decision to act: something which will be a προαίρεσις in the strict sense if it is the outcome of ethical reasoning, and something which will be a προαίρεσις in the broad sense if it is an outcome of technical reasoning. It will be an expression of δίωξις or φυγή, 'I am to pursue this' or 'I am to avoid that'.[1] The same concept of the conclusion of practical reasoning is suggested by the discussion of incontinence in *AE* c, which we shall shortly consider.

It is often maintained by commentators, however, that Aristotle thought of the action itself as being the conclusion of the practical reasoning that leads up to it. They point to a famous passage of the *De Motu Animalium*:

> How is it that thought is sometimes followed by action, sometimes not; sometimes by movement, sometimes not? What happens seems parallel to the case of thinking and reasoning about unchangeable matters. There the end is a piece of theoretical knowledge (for when one thinks of the two premises one thinks of and puts together the conclusion), but here the two premises result in a conclusion which is an action —for example one thinks that all men are to march and that one is a man oneself: straightway one marches; or no men are to march now and that one is a man: straightway one halts. (701a7-15)

Here Aristotle is stressing the immediacy of action upon reasoning. Certainly, once having reasoned out what to do there is no need to enunciate the conclusion in words, aloud or to oneself, before proceeding to act. But Aristotle is not meaning here that there is no such thing as practical reasoning where no

[1] 'I am to pursue' and other 'am to' forms are meant to correspond to the imperatives and gerunds that Aristotle uses (ποιητέον, βαδιστέον, etc.). They are not meant to carry, any more than the Greek expressions do, overtones of duty.

action follows. He goes on immediately to say 'And so one acts in the two cases *provided there is nothing to prevent or to compel'*—if prevention or compulsion took place, that would not mean that the reasoning was inconclusive. The upshot of a piece of practical reasoning may be either an action or a decision to act (which need not, as in the present case, be concerned with immediate action). Aristotle is willing to call a decision to act 'an action', as we see in the very next example he gives:

> Again, I should make a good thing, a house is a good thing; straightway I make a house. I need a covering, a cloak is a covering; I need a cloak. What I need I should make, I need a cloak; I should make a cloak. And the conclusion 'I should make a cloak' is an action.

It is normally only in the case when decisions are not acted on (in the case, for instance of the incontinent) or where action is postponed that there is any point in distinguishing between the act and the decision. Sometimes as above Aristotle makes this point by saying that the conclusion is the action; sometimes, as a few pages later, he says that the two are simultaneous: 'It is almost simultaneously that one thinks one ought to go and that one goes' (702a17).

We have now considered, with reference primarily to the case of technical reasoning, the nature of the various premises and of the conclusion of a piece of practical reasoning. We must now consider, finally, the nature of the transition between premises and conclusion and inquire what is the nature of validity in practical reasoning.

Aristotle sometimes speaks as if the premises of a piece of practical reasoning necessitate its conclusion, and indeed necessitate the agent's acting upon the conclusion. When the universal premise and the other premise come together, he says,

> the soul must at once affirm the conclusion; and in the case of productive reasoning it must immediately act.

But when he says that it is necessary ($\dot{a}\nu\dot{a}\gamma\kappa\eta$) that the soul should affirm and act, he cannot mean that the performance of the appropriate action is necessitated by logical necessity, since a few lines further on he considers the possibility that someone may be prevented or incapacitated from performing the act in spite of having brought the premises together in his mind. But is the drawing of the conclusion necessitated in the way that the conclusion of a piece of theoretical reasoning is necessitated by its premises?

Neither in theoretical nor in practical reasoning is anyone *forced* to draw a conclusion. The way in which theoretical conclusions are necessitated by a valid argument is that if the premises are true then it must be that the conclusion is true. Now in the case of practical inference the goal of the reasoning is the good, just as in the case of theoretical inference the goal of the reasoning is the truth. Consequently, just as the rules of valid argument in the theoretical mode are designed to ensure that in reasoning one will never pass from something which is true to something which is not true, so the criterion for the validity of a practical inference should be that it conforms to a pattern which will never lead from what is good to what is not good. Just as the truth of the premises is communicated to—or, as Aristotle would say, causes—the truth of the conclusion in a valid argument, so the goodness of the initial premise (the goal-premise setting out the desired end) is communicated to the conclusion which is the decision to adopt the means (the προαίρεσις resulting from the deliberation). This is made clear by Aristotle in an important passage of the first book of the *EE*:

> That the end stands in a causal relation to the means sub-ordinate to it is shown by the method of teachers; they prove that the means are severally good by giving a definition of the end, because the end aimed at is a cause: for instance, since to be healthy is so-and-so, necessarily what conduces to health must be so-and-so. What is wholesome is an efficient cause of health; but it is only the cause of its (coming into) existence, it is not the cause of its being a good. No one demonstrates that health is good.

Thus, in the demonstration that, e.g., rubbing is wholesome, goodness attaching to the first premise ('This man is to be healed') is communicated, *via* the intermediate premises, to the conclusion 'So I'll rub him'; just as in the reverse order the rubbing is the efficient cause of the production of health, and the theoretical announcement 'I shall rub him', plus the intermediate medical premises, if true, will yield the true conclusion 'He will be healed'.

It is one thing to set out a criterion for the validity of a piece of practical reasoning, and quite another thing to set out an actual system of rules for discriminating valid from invalid practical inferences. Aristotle did not draw up any such system of rules for practical inference to correspond to and no one else has succeeded in doing so up to the present day. The one thing that is clear is that the rules must be different ones from the rules of theoretical reasoning, or at least be applied in a very different way. This is obvious in Aristotle's own examples. Consider again the familiar cloak syllogism of the *De Motu*:

> I need a covering
> A cloak is a covering
> I need a cloak
> I must make what I need
> I need a cloak
> I should make a cloak. (701a18)

This looks like a piece of reasoning of the following form: 'A is B, C is A, so C is B; B is D, C is B, so C is D.' Here all the premises are indefinite and should therefore be treated as particulars (*Prior Anal.* 26a29, 29b27). This would make the first syllogism—'Some A is B, some C is A, some C is B'—invalid through having two particular premises. There seems no way to make Aristotle's example valid within his own syllogistic. Again the inferences in conditional form illustrated by the medical example in the *Metaphysics* involve transitions of the following type:

> I am to do Y
> If I do X I shall do Y
> So I am to do X.

If this is taken as an instance of the theoretical reasoning pattern q; but if p then q; so p, it illustrates the familiar fallacy of affirming the consequent.

146 *Aristotle's Theory of the Will*

Since, as Aristotle insists, the direction of reasoning in practical matters is the reverse of that in theoretical matters, ('In practical reasonings the end is the beginning' is one of his favourite paradoxical formulations (e.g. *EE* II.11, 1127a20)), it is not difficult to construct goodness-preserving rules. Wherever 'From A infer B' is a sound truth-preserving rule, 'From B infer A' is a sound goodness-preserving rule.[1] But this simple device will not suffice to enable us to develop a formal logic of practical reasoning mirroring theoretical syllogistic and propositional calculus. For truth-preservation differs from goodness-preservation in a fundamental respect. If a proposition is true, then it is not also false; but if a project or proposal or decision is good, that does not exclude its being also, from another point of view, bad. Hence, while truth-preserving rules will exclude falsehood, goodness-preserving rules will not exclude badness.

This fact alone makes the formalisation of practical reasoning an enormously more complicated task than the formalisation of theoretical reasoning; so that we need not wonder that Aristotle did not attempt the task, and that no subsequent philosopher has succeeded in it.

---

[1] I have developed this point, and defended it against objections, in the prolegomena to a formalisation of practical reasoning presented in Kenny, 1975, 70–96.

13. Ethical Reasoning

In Aristotle's ethical writings, though there are many illustrations of technical syllogisms, it is difficult to find a clear example of a worked out piece of ethical inference.[1] Aristotle seems to have thought that the logical structure of ethical reasoning sufficiently resembled that of technical reasoning, so that it was unnecessary to give separate treatment to it. In the present chapter I wish to inquire into the differences between technical and ethical reasoning, as understood by Aristotle, and to consider his reasons for choosing technical syllogisms as his primary illustrations of practical reasoning.

We may start from a problem which is raised by Aristotle's insistence that we do not deliberate about ends. The doctor, we are told, does not deliberate whether he shall heal a patient. But may not the doctor be tempted to stay in bed when called out at midnight, or wonder whether the patient would not be better off dead, or perhaps even deliberately worsen the patient's condition in the interests of medical research? I think it is clear that Aristotle's answer would be that such deliberation would be ethical, not technical deliberation: the doctor would be deliberating not *qua* doctor, but *qua* moral agent, or if deliberating *qua* doctor, then *qua* subscriber to the Hippocratic Oath rather than *qua* possessor of a certain technical skill. When we are told, then, that the doctor does not deliberate about whether to heal a patient, what is meant is that any such deliberation is not an exercise of medical skill.

Aristotle often says that the science of medicine, like all sciences, is a science of contraries (e.g. *AE* A. 1, 1129a12ff): it is productive of disease as well as of health, giving the power

[1] The nearest to such an example occurs in *AE* c.3, and will be discussed at length in the next chapter.

to kill as well as to cure. How is this to be reconciled with the statement that the doctor, *qua* doctor, does not deliberate whether to heal? The answer must surely be that though the doctor may have to decide whether to use his medical skill one way or the other, the process of reaching *this* decision is not itself a use of the skill, and therefore not a bit of technical deliberation. Further knowledge of medicine will not help a man to decide whether to his use knowledge of medicine to kill or cure.

In giving examples of medical syllogisms, Aristotle naturally chooses the standard case where the end assumed by the doctor is to heal. But technical reasoning could equally well be illustrated by the opposite case. 'A doctor does not deliberate whether he shall poison, but taking that end for granted, investigates by what means he can most easily and effectively poison.' The important point about technical deliberation is that it must always start from an initial premise which is not arrived at as a result of previous technical reasoning. The initial premise might be the expression of a temporary whim, a momentary craving for pleasure, say (cf. 1142b17); or it may be the result of ethical deliberation, forming part of an overall plan of the good life.[1]

The difference between ethical reasoning and technical reasoning is fourfold. First, though ethical deliberation, like technical deliberation, can be said to be a search for means to an end, the means-end relationship must be interpreted in a much broader sense than in the simple medical examples by which technical reasoning has been illustrated. Secondly, the initial premise of ethical reasoning is of a different kind, and is acquired in a different manner, from the initial premise of technical reasoning. Thirdly, the ultimate premises of ethical reasoning are acquired not by sense-perception, as in many cases of technical reasoning, but by ethical intuition. Fourthly, the conclusion of a piece of ethical reasoning is linked to ethical conduct in a way much more complicated than that in which technical reasoning is linked to technical execution.

---

[1] In the case of the doctor, what is the result of ethical deliberation is the decision to exercise the profession of medicine. That health is a good is not something which is the result of any kind of deliberation or proof (*EE* 1.8, 1218b22).

These four differences between the two kinds of reasoning are four differences between skill (τέχνη) and wisdom (φρόνησις). For wisdom is essentially the capacity to produce and execute correct ethical syllogisms, just as τέχνη is the capacity to produce and execute correct technical syllogisms. Let us examine in turn these four differences between skill and wisdom, between technical and ethical deliberation.

Deliberation, Aristotle has frequently told us, concerns not the end, but the means (see p. 77 above). The Greek expression traditionally translated 'means' is literally 'the things towards the end' (τὰ πρὸς τὸ τέλος). In recent years it has rightly often been emphasised that this expression has a far broader sense than at first appears: it includes not only instrumental means which are distinct from the end, but constitutive means which are in some sense parts of the end.[1] Among the 'means' to health in this sense will be not only such things as drugs and massage, but also such things as a good digestion and healthy kidneys.[2] Among the 'means' to happiness in this sense will be not only such things as money and power, but such things as the enjoyment of aesthetic pleasure and the exercise of power in glorious deeds. I have used, and will continue to use, the traditional translation of τὰ πρὸς τὸ τέλος; but 'ways and means' might be a better translation than 'means', since many of Aristotle's 'means' to happiness are in fact ways of being happy.

Because ποίησις is concerned with the production of ends distinct from the process of production while πρᾶξις is concerned with the performance of actions which are valuable in themselves, the relationship of instrumental means to ends is the preponderant one in technical reasoning, while the relationship of constituent means to ends is the dominant one in ethical reasoning. To choose to do X as a result of ethical deliberation is both a decision to do X as a means to happiness, and to do X for its own sake, because it is a splendid or admirable thing to do (it is καλόν). Aristotle uses both formulations, and there is

[1] This is insisted on, for instance, by Hardie (1968, 256) and Cooper (1975, 19ff).
[2] Aristotle recognises this explicitly in the *Metaphysics* Z passage on practical reasoning quoted above (1032b26–9).

no inconsistency between the two. A happy life, for him, just is a life made up of splendid and admirable actions.[1]

Aristotle judges rightly that the difference between instrumental and constitutive means is not sufficient to make a difference in the logical form of practical reasoning. The reasoning from goal to action follows the same pattern whether the conditionals which occur in the intermediate premises express a means-end relationship, a part-whole relationship, or even a relationship of logical equivalence. There is no difference of logical form between 'If I rub him, he will be heated' and 'If I spend my life in philosophical contemplation, I will be happy'.

The initial premise of a technical syllogism is concerned with a particular goal, such as health or victory. The initial premise of an ethical syllogism sets out an ideal of human good, an overall plan of life. It is this which is referred to in the passage which misbegot the expression 'practical syllogism' (see p. 111 above). 'Those syllogisms which contain the starting point of πρᾶξις run "since the end, or the highest good, is such-and-such" ' (1144a29-b1). We are not, in the *Ethics*, given an instance of a virtuous initial premise: unless we say that the whole *Ethics* is meant to provide one. But in *AE* c we are given the vicious initial premise of the intemperate man: 'The highest good is the unremitting pursuit of each pleasure that offers' (1146b24, 1151a23).

In the *De Anima* Aristotle tells us that the universal premise of a piece of reasoning leading to action is of the form 'Such and such a kind of man should do such and such a kind of act' (434a16). This formulation would fit both technical and ethical reasoning. In ethical reasoning it would take such forms as 'A just and honourable man should pay his debts'; in technical reasoning it might take the form of an example suggested by Professor Anscombe 'Pregnant women should watch their weight', though if so it would have to be subsidiary to some more general universal about the nature of health (see above p. 131).

One of the examples of practical reasoning in the *De Motu* runs thus (701a7ff):

[1] This formulation fits the *EE* better than the *NE*; see below p. 153f, and Kenny, 1978, 190ff.

I ought to make something good
A house is good

after which, we are told, 'Straightway I make a house'. This
rather breathless syllogism does not seem to be a technical
syllogism belonging to the art of housebuilding; for it does not
begin with the end or goal of housebuilding. The initial premise
of a technical housebuilding syllogism would be the plan of a
house (as a theory of health initiates medical reasoning). What
we have here, it seems, is something unique in Aristotle: an
instance of the linking of ethical and practical reasoning. It
can, at least, be so interpreted if it is understood as part of the
deliberation of a rich philanthropist wondering what he should
do with his money.

The initial premise of a piece of technical reasoning is something which can be learnt: a theory of health, for instance, is
communicated by teaching (*EE* 1.8, 1218b16). But wisdom
cannot be taught in the way that a technical skill can: the
initial premise of practical reasoning is something which it
takes a special quality of character to see the truth of (*AE* B,
1144a44). Wisdom, which is defined as a truth-attaining, ratiocinative quality concerning what is good for human beings, has
as one of its major constituents the intuitive grasp of the initial
premise of ethical reasoning, the theory of human good
(1142b34). Wisdom is excellence in ethical deliberation: it has
two intuitive elements, corresponding to the intuition of the
initial and ultimate premises, and one ratiocinative element,
corresponding to the transition from premises to conclusion.
The two intuitive elements are each called *νοῦς*; the ratiocinative element is called *εὐβουλία*.

In a theoretical discipline like geometry, according to
Aristotle, intuition comes in at two points: first, in the appreciation of first indemonstrable principles or axioms; secondly, in
the realisation that particular individuals are instances of
generalisations (*AE* B, 1140b31ff, 1142a29, 1143b6). Similarly
with intuition in practical matters:

Νοῦς is concerned with extremes in both directions: it is *νοῦς*
and not reasoning whose objects are primary terms and
ultimate particulars. There is one *νοῦς* of the unchangeable
L

and primary terms in the realm of demonstration, and
another of the ultimate and contingent element, and of the
other (*sc.* of the initial) premise in practical reasoning; for
these are the principles of the wherefore; for universals come
from particulars, and for these you have to have a perception
which is νοῦς.

The νοῦς which deals with the universal premise of practical
reasoning corresponds to the intuitive understanding of
speculative axioms, since axioms in mathematical reasoning
play the same role as the wherefore, or οὗ ἕνεκα, in practical
reasoning (*AE* c, 1151a17). The νοῦς which deals with the
ultimate and contingent elements will be the intuitive perception of the ethically relevant features of particular situations.
This sort of intuition is necessary both for the exercise, and for
the acquisition, of an overall theory of the good life as consisting
in the deployment of the moral and intellectual virtues. For
instance, a just appreciation of the needs of others will be
needed both for a child to acquire a correct concept of generosity by studying the actions of generous men and also in the
exercise of his own generosity by a mature and virtuous adult.[1]
Thus, ethical reasoning will differ from technical reasoning to
the extent that intuition plays the role in ethical reasoning that
learning from teachers and sense-perception plays in technical
reasoning.[2]

The final difference to be remarked between ethical and

[1] Just as, in geometry, an ability to spot the geometrically relevant
figures of a diagram is necessary both in the initial acquisition of the axioms
via the teacher's visual aids, and in the construction of figures by a graduate
geometer going about his work.

Because intuition is necessary at both stages, it is possible to reconcile the
apparently conflicting accounts of the role of intuition in ethical reasoning
given by Monan (1968, 74–8) and Cooper (1975, 42).

[2] There is a close parallel between the structure of σοφία (the virtue of the
scientific part of the rational soul) and φρόνησις (the virtue of the deliberative part). Each consists of νοῦς-plus-λόγος-plus-νοῦς: in the case of σοφία
this is intuition of axioms plus ἐπιστήμη plus intuition of particulars; in
φρόνησις intuition of the nature of the good for man plus εὐβουλία plus
intuition of particulars.

My interpretation of 1143a35ff is controversial. It is expounded at greater
length and defended in Kenny, 1978, 170–3.

technical reason concerns the relationship between conclusion
and action. A doctor may reason out impeccably how to cure
a patient: he may fail to act on his conclusion for a variety of
reasons (e.g. because he is lazy, or avaricious). His failure to
act does not count against his possession of the skill, however
much it may count against his character or moral standing.
Failure to carry out the ethical deliberation characteristic of
wisdom, however, is itself evidence against the genuine possession
of wisdom by the deliberator (*AE* B, 1140b22; *AE* c.9, 1152a6).

Thus, the transition from the conclusion to the action is more
intimately related to the nature of ethical reasoning than the
execution of a technical plan is to the nature of technical
planning. A full treatment of ethical reasoning therefore must
include a consideration of the way in which the link between
reason and action may break down. To this the next chapter
will be devoted: but first, one final complication about the
order of premises in ethical reasoning must be mentioned.

In the προαίρεσις of every virtuous man there will be a universal premise of the form: the virtue of X (e.g. of temperance),
which is of such-and-such a nature, is to be pursued. But in the
final chapter of the *Eudemian Ethics* we learn that there are two
different ways in which this universal may be present: either as
the ultimate universal or as itself derived from a further
universal. Only those for whom this is the ultimate universal
are perfectly virtuous, are καλοὶ κἀγαθοί.[1]

> There are some who think one should have virtue, but only
> for the sake of the natural goods. Such men are good men (for
> the natural goods are good for them) but they do not have
> perfect virtue (καλοκἀγαθίαν): for their noble qualities are
> not acquired for their own sake. The perfectly virtuous
> acquire them and also make these the object of their purpose[2]

---

[1] One might say that the ultimate universal concerns the pursuit and
nature of happiness, so that it would be more correct to mark the distinction
between perfect and imperfect virtue in terms of the penultimate premise.
This would be possible; but it is not necessary, since to set something up as
one's idea of happiness is for Aristotle the same thing as to pursue it as the
ultimate goal of one's practical reasoning.

[2] The MSS here read οὐ γὰρ ὑπάρχει αὐτοῖς τὰ καλὰ δι' αὐτὰ καὶ
προαιροῦνται καλοὶ κἀγαθοί, which does not make sense. Ross and Rackham

—not only that, but things which by nature are not noble but merely good become noble to them: for things become noble when people's motives in doing and choosing them are noble. (1248b40-9a8)

The natural goods are such things as health and strength and wealth: these are good in themselves, but may be harmful, good, or noble depending on the characters of the persons to whom they fall. To an evil man they are positively harmful, as a robust diet is to an unhealthy person. To a good man they are good, for he will not abuse them. But there is an imperfection in the virtue of a man who, though he practises the virtues and does not abuse the gifts of nature, values the virtues only because they contribute to preserving health and strength and maximising wealth. (Readers of Kant are reminded of the grocer who practises honesty simply because it is financially the best policy.) Perfect virtue demands a reversal of these priorities: health and wealth are themselves to be valued because of the splendid and noble deeds they enable their possessor to perform. The bodily and external goods themselves share in the nobility of their possessor: that is to say, it is a fine and splendid thing that someone whose heart is set on virtue and not on riches should be rich enough to exercise his virtues to the full (1249a8–17).[1]

---

emend to καλὰ κἀγαθά, which gives sense at the cost of an intolerably clumsy construction. A simpler emendation which makes better sense and a smoother reading is to insert ἅ after δι' αὐτά. The translation above assumes this emendation.

[1] The *NE* parallel to this final chapter appears to be the brief remark at 1105a32 that virtuous actions must be chosen for their own sake. Both ethics make the point on several occasions in their treatment of particular virtues (*EE* III, 1229a2ff, 1230a29–32; *NE* 3, 1115b20–21, 1117a5, 1119b16, etc.). (As these passages show, virtue is chosen for its own sake, and ὅτι καλόν: the two are not the same thing, since e.g. pleasure could be chosen for its own sake, without being chosen ὅτι καλόν—that is precisely what the incontinent as opposed to the intemperate does.)

14. The Breakdown of Ethical Reasoning

The fullest single treatment of practical inference by Aristotle occurs in the third chapter of the common book c, where the topic is the breakdown of the connection between reason and action which takes place in the case of incontinence. To show the different ways in which the breakdown can take place, Aristotle carefully dismantles the mechanism of the practical syllogism and shows in turn how each of the parts can malfunction. To the logical distinctions between conclusions and premises of various types he adds a distinction between degrees of actuality, and a theory about the influence of physiology on mental operations, in order to present an account of incontinence which will preserve the element of truth in the Socratic dictum that no one does wrong except in ignorance without clashing with the universally accepted opinion that men sometimes do what they know they should not.[1]

Consider the following piece of practical reasoning, suggested by the passage 1147a4–6:

Dry food is good for any man
Chicken is dry   I am a man
This is chicken
So I'll have some.

We may suppose that the reasoning is followed by eating some of the chicken.

[1] I have discussed the chapter at length in my paper 'The Practical Syllogism and Incontinence' (1966). The principal conclusions of that paper still seem to me correct, and where this is so I merely state them in the present text without further argument. Where I have modified my position since 1966 in the light of further criticism, and in the light of the conviction that *AE* c belongs with the *EE*, I have marked the differences in footnotes. The main lines of my 1966 argument have been endorsed by Rowe (1971, 115–20).

The premise 'Dry food is good for any man' Aristotle calls the universal premise. Since it is his constant teaching that deliberation starts from the assumption of a goal, and since no goal is explicitly mentioned in the reasoning, we must assume that dry food is good for (συμφέρει) men in the sense of conducive to health, so that the tacit goal is health; the universal premise is simply part of a general theory of health such as that mentioned in *EE* 1 at 1218b18, 'Since to be in health is so and so, so and so must needs be what conduces to it'. The universal premise, as Aristotle points out, contains two universal terms 'dry food' and 'any man'. This is a general feature of Aristotelian practical reasoning, which involves showing that the deliberator falls under a certain description, and that a certain action or object falls under a certain description.[1] It is the presence of generalisations of this degree of abstraction which makes the difference between the animal pursuit of desire (which can be, without inappropriate anthropomorphism, verbalised in *singular* sentences such as 'I need a drink', 'This is a drink'; cf. *DMA* 701a31) and the practical reasoning characteristic of rational human beings.

All the rest of the deliberation, up to the conclusion, is called by Aristotle 'the particular premise': it is clearly a composite one, consisting of three atomic premises, one of which, 'Chicken is dry', is in fact a universally quantified one, though containing a universal of less extent than the one 'dry food' which occurs in the official universal premise. There seems to be no limit in theory to the number of atomic premises that can be combined to make the particular premise: a parallel passage in the *De Anima* mentions two, and a parallel passage in *AE* B.7 suggests four.[2] The atomic premise 'I am a man' is not one which would

[1] Thus in the *De Anima* we are told that a universal judgment in practical reasoning 'tells us that such and such a kind of man should do such and such a kind of act' (434a16).

[2] In the *De Anima* passage just cited, the particular premise is 'This is an act of the kind meant, and I am a person of the type intended' (434a18). The passage at *AE* B.7, 1141b18 suggests the following reasoning:

Digestible meat is healthy for any man
Light meats are digestible   I am a man
Chicken is light
This is chicken   So I'll have some.

normally give ground for any trouble in deliberation (cf. *DMA* 701a26; *NE* 3, 1117a7); but the deliberation concerning the description applied to the agent might be more elaborate than in this artificially simple example: e.g. 'No civil servant should write letters to the newspaper; a teacher is a civil servant; I am a teacher . . .'

In the passage 1147a4–6 from which the above example is taken, no conclusion is in fact drawn, since the passage is intended to illustrate not the successful operation of practical reasoning but its breakdown. But a few lines further down he describes reasoning brought to a conclusion. When the universal and the other premise[1] come together, he says,

> the soul must at once affirm the conclusion; and in the case of technical reasoning it must immediately act. Thus, if one must taste everything sweet, and this is sweet (this being one of the individual terms), then a man who can act and is not prevented must simultaneously act accordingly. (1147a27–28)[2]

Since Aristotle specifies that this is a technical syllogism, we are presumably to imagine it as forming part of the practical reasoning of e.g. a pastrycook.[3] Expanded accordingly, it will run:

(It was this passage which suggested using 'chicken' as a substitution for the variable τοιόνδε at 1147a4).

[1] Aristotle here calls it the individual (καθ' ἕκαστον) premise. This expression really fits only the conjunct of the final atomic premises (such as 'I am a man and this is chicken' or 'I am a pastrycook and this is sweet').

[2] As in my 1966 paper, in the sentence ἀνάγκη τὸ συμπερανθὲν ἔνθα μὲν φάναι τὴν ψυχήν, ἐν δὲ ταῖς ποιητικαῖς πράττειν εὐθύς I take the ἔνθα μέν and ἐν δέ not to be an instance of ἔνθα μέν . . . ἔνθα δέ (as it is commonly taken by commentators, making an irrelevant contrast between theoretical and practical reasoning) but to make the contrast between what happens immediately (ἔνθα) in all cases, and what happens further in some cases (the ποιητικαί cases). But I now take ποιητικαί to mark the usual contrast between ποίησις and πρᾶξις: Aristotle is contrasting the straightforward case of technical reasoning, where there is no occasion for the conflict of reason and desire, with the case he is about to consider of incontinence, where desire interferes between the drawing of a practical conclusion and its enactment. My earlier suggestion, that ποιητικαί referred to positive conclusions (διώκειν τοῦτο) as opposed to negative (κωλυτικαί) ones, such as φεύγειν τοῦτο, now seems to me fanciful.

[3] This would explain why Aristotle insists that 'This is sweet' concerns only *one* of the individual terms.

> Any pastrycook should taste everything sweet
> I am a pastrycook   This is a sweet
> So I'll taste it (tasting it).

The conclusions of these technical syllogisms 'So I'll have some chicken' 'So I'll taste this sweet' are examples of judgments arising as a result of deliberation—they thus fulfil the criterion for being προαιρέσεις in accordance with the definitions of *NE* 3 and *EE* 11. They are the expression of deliberative desire which is the result of the coalescing of desire (to be healthy, to do one's job as a pastrycook) with the reasoning set out in the premises.[1]

In the light of the discussion in B.2, however, such decisions would not be προαιρέσεις ἁπλῶς, would not be purposes in the fullest sense, unless they could trace their ancestry of practical reasoning back up to a universal premise concerning the good for man as such. Aristotle gives us one such example of a universal ethical premise: the universal of the intemperate man, which is 'A man should always pursue the present pleasure' (1146b20). Putting this universal premise together with the fragment of practical reasoning which Aristotle offers in his discussion of incontinence at 1147a32–34 we obtain the following practical syllogism:

> A man should always pursue the present pleasure
> (I am a man)   Sweet things are pleasant
>   Here is a sweet thing
>   So I'll taste it.

This is an ethical, not merely technical syllogism, since it is concerned with putting into effect a conception of the good life.

In fact Aristotle never gives a fully worked out concrete example of an ethical syllogism, and the passage which suggested the above example does not specify the universal premise. It runs as follows:

> So when there is present a universal premise forbidding tasting, and another saying 'Every sweet thing is pleasant and

[1] Compare the language of the present passage ὅταν δὲ μία γένεται ἐξ αὐτῶν, ἀνάγκη τὸ συμπερανθέν . . . φάναι τὴν ψυχήν with that of *EE* 11's description of προαίρεσις as being δόξα καὶ ὄρεξις, ὅταν ἐκ τοῦ βουλεύσασθαι συμπερανθῶσιν (1227a4–5).

this is sweet' (this premise being operative), and when appetite happens to be present, then it says 'Avoid this', but appetite drives on; because each part of the soul is capable of setting us in motion. (1147a32–34)

It is a pity that Aristotle does not spell out the universal premise for us; but we can reconstruct it to a certain extent.[1] First, we know that it must be the universal premise characteristic of σωφροσύνη or temperance: for the case is meant to illustrate the practical reasoning of the incontinent man, and we know that the incontinent man shares the principles of the temperate man. Now the aim of the temperate man is to seek the mean in the bodily pleasures of touch and taste (*EE* III, 1230b21–31a38; *NE* 3, 1117b23–19b18). Consequently the universal premise will be concerned with the avoidance of excessive gustatory pleasure. It will be concerned with the avoidance of tastes precisely *qua* pleasant (not, say, *qua* unhealthy: that would be the concern of a different type of practical reasoning). Thus— and this is the second important thing we can say with confidence in reconstructing the reasoning—it is a premise which in conjunction with the information provided by the particular premise, that sweets are pleasant and here is a sweet,[2] leads to the concluding προαίρεσις 'Avoid this' or 'Don't taste this'.[3]

[1] In my 1966 article I suggested that the universal was something like 'Taste nothing pleasant'. This suggestion was prompted by an excessive desire to make the form of practical reasoning conform to patterns which would be valid in theoretical reasoning. I now think such a universal prohibition too sweeping to be what Aristotle had in mind; but I remain convinced of the main point, that the premise is concerned with the avoidance of *pleasure* as such, and not with the avoidance of sweetness, unhealthiness, or whatever.

[2] I have given reasons in my 1966 article, which seem to me conclusive, for regarding the 'other' which says πᾶν γλυκὺ ἡδύ, τουτὶ δὲ γλυκύ as being not another *universal*, but another premise; one which is 'particular' in the sense in which 'Chicken is dry and this is chicken' is.

[3] Reasoning of this ascetic kind is nowadays so uncommon that it is often difficult to convince contemporary Aristotelians that this is the kind of argument Aristotle had in mind. But while Aristotle does admit that there can be excessive abstention from bodily pleasure (the vice of ἀναισθησία) his criterion for the appropriate pursuit of bodily goods and sensual pleasures is a very rigorous one: 'Whatever choice of possession of natural goods—

Since the reasoning is imagined as taking place in an incontinent man, the προαίρεσις which is the conclusion of the deliberation is not acted upon. The purpose of spelling out the different stages of the reasoning was to throw light on the problem whether the incontinent acts knowingly or in error. Once we have seen the practical syllogism set out we realise that the question is not a simple one: there are several different items of information involved, and the incontinent may be aware of some of them and not of others. For his purpose, Aristotle does not need to spell out the universal premise in detail, because he agrees with popular opinion against Socrates that the incontinent man is aware of this principle throughout. He agrees, however, with Socrates, that there *is* a certain kind of ἄγνοια or failure of knowledge in the incontinent. In order to reconcile his agreement with Socrates with his agreement with the popular opinion he needs not only to distinguish different kinds of premises in practical reasoning, but also different degrees of the possession and exercise of knowledge.

Aristotle often distinguishes between *using* a piece of knowledge (e.g. speaking Greek) and merely *having* it (being a Greek-speaker, but currently engaged in speaking English or silently digging potatoes) (e.g. *De Anima* 417a26ff). He here also distinguishes between the state of someone who knows Greek and is awake (so that if someone spoke to him in Greek he would at once understand) and someone who has learnt Greek and is asleep: a distinction, we might say, between *having* and *half-having* a piece of knowledge.[1]

Not having, half-having, having, and using are four points on

---

health and strength, wealth, friends and the like—will most conduce to the contemplation of God is best: this is the finest criterion. But any standard of living which either through excess or defect hinders the service and contemplation of God is bad. This applies also to the soul: for the soul the ideal standard is to have the minimum awareness of the irrational part of the soul, *qua* irrational' (*EE* VIII, 1249b17–23). Enjoyment of pleasures of touch and taste not necessitated by the rational pursuit of other goals would presumably count as 'awareness of the irrational part of the soul, *qua* irrational'.

[1] What I, for brevity, call 'half-having' Aristotle calls 'having and not having' (1147a12); the scholastics called it *habitus ligatus* in contrast to *habitus solutus*.

a scale of increasing actualisation of potentiality. If we name the points on the scale not from the point of view of the possessor of knowledge, but of the item of knowledge itself, we can speak of the knowledge as being absent, half-present, present, and operative. Aristotle uses both terminologies in the present passage. We now have a fourfold possibility instead of the simple Socratic alternative of 'knowingly' or 'in error'.

What is the difference, then, between a piece of knowledge being merely present, and being actually operative? In the case of practical knowledge, an item is operative if it thrusts towards action. What this metaphorical expression means will differ from case to case, according to the nature of the individual items in question. A practical generalisation, a universal premise, will be operative when consequences are drawn from it that are more particular and therefore closer to practical implementation. (Thus the generalisation 'Dry food is good' is operative when it leads to the realisation that 'Chicken is good'). A particular premise will be operative when it leads to a practical conclusion being drawn (e.g. when 'This is chicken' leads to the decision 'So I'll eat some'). A practical conclusion, in its turn, is operative when it is actually acted upon: when, having said 'So I'll eat some', the diner actually tucks in.

Aristotle seems to envisage two principal kinds of breakdown in practical reasoning in cases of incontinence. In one case, the reasoning does not reach its conclusion because one of the intermediate premises is missing or remains inoperative; in the other case, the reasoning goes through to its conclusion, and it is the conclusion which remains inoperative. The first case is hinted at in the passage 1147a4–10;[1] the second case is spelt out in detail in 1147a24–1147b1.[2] The first case corresponds to impetuous incontinence, and the second to weak-willed incontinence, as described in a later passage of book c (1150b19–23):

Of incontinence one kind is impetuosity, another weakness.

[1] Only hinted at, because the passage concerns a technical syllogism and is not explicitly discussing ἀκρασία.

[2] In which he explicitly insists that the intermediate premise operates (a33).

For some men after deliberating fail, because of passion, to keep to the conclusions of their deliberation; others because of their failure to deliberate are driven by their passion.

In neither case is there any failure to operate on the part of the universal premise: Aristotle always attributes the breakdown elsewhere.

Simply to describe incontinence as the failure to act on a premise or a conclusion is unilluminating: it seems to set rather than to solve the problem in question. Aristotle's own explanation of incontinence depends upon his distinction between having and half-having. Half-having, he observes, is compatible with a pseudo-exercise of knowledge: drunks, sleepers, and madmen may mouth the words of Empedocles without that being a genuine exercise of philosophical knowledge. Hence, the fact that the incontinent man enunciates the decision 'avoid this' need not mean that he fully 'has' the 'knowledge'[1] expressed in these words: he may only half-have it, like a person talking in his sleep (1147a16-18).

Now if a person has a piece of knowledge but does not exercise it, or if he half-has a piece of knowledge and at most pseudo-exercises it, is he rightly described as ἀγνοῶν? The answer is not given explicitly in *AE* c: but the main lines of an answer are laid down in *EE* II.9:

Since science or knowledge is of two sorts, one the having and one the using of knowledge, a man who has but does not use knowledge may in a manner justly be described as ἀγνοῶν, but in another manner not justly: e.g. if his non-use of his knowledge is due to negligence. Similarly, a person might be blamed for not having a piece of knowledge, if it is something easy and necessary, and his not having it is the result of negligence or pleasure or pain. (1225b14-16)

---

[1] As we move down the practical syllogism from universal to decision the word 'knowledge', ἐπιστήμη, becomes less and less apposite, and δόξα more so. Aristotle was aware of this, but rightly argues that the difference between the two terms is unimportant for the immediate purpose (1146b24). Even for the universal δόξα is the more appropriate word for him, reasoning about contingent matters being the function of the δοξαστικόν (1140b26).

We learn from this on the one hand that mere non-exercise in itself does not count as a case of ἄγνοια (there must be some reason for the non-exercise other than lack of willingness to put the knowledge to work); and on the other hand that the not having a piece of knowledge—and so presumably *a fortiori* the merely half-having a piece of knowledge—does not necessarily excuse from blame. Now in the cases of incontinence described by Aristotle in *AE* c.3 the agent is in a state of half-having with respect to either a premise or a conclusion: his failure to act on his reasoning is not merely a matter of inadvertence, even of negligent inadvertence. Hence he can justly be said to be ἀγνοῶν. But because his ἄγνοια is due to appetite—it is appetite which makes him merely half-have the knowledge— he acts merely ἀγνοῶν, not δι' ἄγνοιαν, and because he lacks knowledge 'as a result of pleasure' he is blameworthy. For the states which result in the half-having of knowledge are not necessarily states which excuse from the failure to apply knowledge: madness no doubt does so, drunkenness clearly does not, and sleep might in some cases and sometimes not (it would not, for instance, excuse a sentry's inability to recognise and respond to a password). Incontinence is compared to these states not in respect of its moral evaluation, but in respect of its physical mechanism. Aristotle clearly thought that sensual desire interferes with the operation of ethical principles through a chain of physical causation analogous to the action of a drug:

The explanation of how the error is dissolved and the incontinent man again becomes a knower is the same as in the case of a man drunk or asleep and is not peculiar to this condition; we must go to the physiologists for it. (1147b6–9)[1]

---

[1] I used to think that this passage must be out of place, because I thought the immediately preceding passage left no room for error, since the conclusion 'Avoid this' is actually drawn. I now realise that even in this case there is a minimum degree of ἄγνοια: the conclusion, though drawn, is only half-had as a piece of knowledge. The text of *AE* c now seems to me to be perfectly in order, and the reorganisations proposed by scholars to be quite unnecessary. Rowe (1971, 119) shows that if 1147b6–9 is misplaced, then so is 1147b9–12; and he says very reasonably, 'There is no limit to the potential madness of an editor; but when we do not even know whether he existed or not, it should not be too easily assumed that he was mad.'

Having painstakingly detailed the elements of his account of incontinence, Aristotle can now go on to claim that he has preserved the truth implicit in Socrates' rejection of the entire possibility of ἀκρασία:

> Since the last proposition is an opinion about a perceptible matter and is something which controls action, and since it is this which the man either does not have while he is in a state of passion, or has in the sense in which having knowledge did not mean knowing but only saying, like a drunken man babbling Empedocles, and since the last term is neither universal nor as scientific as the universal, what Socrates was trying to maintain actually seems to be correct: for it is not as a result of so-called knowledge proper that incontinence occurs, nor is it knowledge proper that is dragged about by passion. (1147a9–17)

Commentators have often argued about the meaning of the words τελευταῖα πρότασις. Some, arguing from the commonest meaning of πρότασις, have claimed that it meant 'final premise'; others,[1] arguing from the demands of the context, have claimed that it meant 'conclusion'. In fact, it means 'last proposition' and what it refers to differs from case to case: it refers to the point at which the reasoning of the incontinent man breaks down. In some cases this is a premise; in other cases it is a conclusion; in each case it is the proposition whose absence, or whose ineffectiveness, is the cause of the incontinence. Smith, an impetuous incontinent who subscribes to the principle that one should not seduce other men's wives, may rush off to bed with Joan after a party without stopping to ascertain that she is married: in his case the proposition that is missing is 'This is Jones's wife'. A less impetuous incontinent might have ascertained this fact, but been undeterred: in such cases this premise is present but perhaps not effective (the conclusion 'So I'll leave her alone' is not drawn), or if it is effective, the conclusion in its turn is ineffective (the resolution is made but not kept). The point which enables Aristotle to claim to be an

---

[1] Including myself in 1966.

ally of Socrates is the fact that the universal premise[1] never fails to be effective in the cases he describes. For such a premise to be 'dragged about like a slave' it would have to be either prevented from being operative, down-graded from presence to half-presence, or misused to an evil end. But in none of Aristotle's examples does this happen. It is not misused: it is not the universal premise of σωφροσύνη, but the δόξα of the αἰσθητικόν 'Sweets are pleasant and this is a sweet' which galvanised the sweet-toothed incontinent into misconduct. It is not inoperative: in all the examples there is a lower-level generalisation to insulate the universal premise from responsibility for the breakdown (e.g. even the sweet-tooth can draw the consequence 'Excessive sweets are to be avoided'). Nor is there any suggestion that it is rendered only half-present by desire in the way in which scientific knowledge is rendered only half-present by drunkenness.

It might be thought that all Aristotle has done is to provide a picture of a mental mechanism with no real explanatory value. How, for instance, when a man commits adultery who believes that adultery is wrong, do we decide whether it was the universal 'Never commit adultery' or the particular 'This is Jones's wife' that was inoperative? Is not Aristotle's solution to the problem of incontinence just an illusion generated by his mechanistic theory of mental operations?

There is no doubt that Aristotle did delude himself with fanciful mechanisms to explain voluntary movement,[2] but his account of the practical reasoning of the incontinent man can easily be separated from its imagined hardware. The criteria by which we decide whether a person subscribes to a general ethical principle are more varied and more diffuse than those by which we decide whether someone really appreciates a particular fact about his present circumstances and whether he really means to act upon a particular decision he enunciates. A man, we might say, has a whole lifetime to show in his

---

[1] The 'so-called knowledge proper' (ἡ κυρίως ἐπιστήμη εἶναι δοκοῦσα) —i.e. what Socrates would call knowledge, but what Aristotle himself would strictly not call ἐπιστήμη, since this must be not only universal, but concerned with non-contingent matters.

[2] See, for instance, *De Motu Animalium*, chapters 7–10 (701a8–703b2).

behaviour whether or not he believes in a universal proposition
of the kind which figures in Aristotelian practical reasonings: as
the propositions become more particular and more immediately
concerned with present action, it is current behaviour which
becomes more and more central as criterial evidence for the
acceptance of the proposition. Since criteria for the acceptance
of the general proposition may be fulfilled without the criteria
for the acceptance of the particular proposition, it makes sense
to speak of the general proposition being present or active
while the particular is not. Smith's attitude to other men's
wives, in general, may show that he is no believer in adultery,
even though his behaviour towards Joan may not be that of a
man who really treats her as Jones's wife; but even if he seduces
her, later remorse may show that he does indeed subscribe to
the proposition 'Joan is Jones's wife'. It is only when we reach
a decision like 'Avoid this now' where there is only one single
behavioural criterion for sincerity in the utterance; and this in
the case of the incontinent is *ex hypothesi* lacking. Here we have
the clash between the verbal criterion for what the person
believes (he says he is not to do it) and the behavioural criterion
(he goes on to do it) which was precisely what Aristotle's
distinction between having and half-having was introduced to
take account of.

The conclusion of the practical reasoning, the 'Pursue this'
or 'Avoid that' which gives expression to the προαίρεσις is,
according to the account of *EE* ii and *AE* b.2, the expression of
both a δόξα and an ὄρεξις. Thus, Aristotle has an answer to the
criticisms made by many commentators in the spirit of Ross's
remark: 'What is missing in his formal theory is the recognition
that incontinence is due not to failure of knowledge but to
weakness of will' (1949, 224). Since προαίρεσις is a combination
of desire and belief, ἄγνοια affecting the προαίρεσις is a very
special kind of ἄγνοια: the inoperativeness of the practical
conclusion is the inoperativeness of a desire as well as the
inoperativeness of a belief; and since the ὄρεξις in question is
one derived by reasoning from the original βούλησις or intellectual desire for the end, the inoperativeness of this desire *is* a
weakness of the will.

CONCLUSION

We have compared and combined the elements of a theory of the will to be found in Aristotle's ethical writings, the *NE*, the *EE* and the *AE*. In conclusion we may set out briefly the results of our inquiry in their bearing on the question of the relationship between the different treatises and the development of Aristotle's ethical doctrine.

We have seen that in their main lines the accounts of voluntariness, purposive choice, and practical reasoning to be found in the *NE* and *EE* resemble each other closely in substance if not always in terminology. We see also that in almost every case where there is a significant difference between the *NE* and the *EE* the *AE* resembles the *EE* more closely than it resembles the *NE*.

Thus, in the account of voluntariness both the *AE* and the *EE*, unlike the *NE*, make a distinction between its being in our power to do an act and its being in our power whether to do or not to do an act: the distinction which lies at the origin of the traditional notion of liberty of indifference. The *AE* and the *EE*, in their account of force, unlike the *NE*, allow that some natural processes, though unforced, are neither voluntary nor involuntary, and both offer the same examples of genuine force. The *AE* and the *EE*, in their treatment of error, make a distinction between the kind of error which is relevant to voluntariness and the kind which is merely incidental: a distinction which is omitted from the *NE*. Neither the *EE* nor the *AE* introduce the question of subsequent remorse or delight as relevant to the voluntariness of action in error: a question which is treated in the *NE* as an important one. The *AE* makes an explicit reference back to a previous treatment of voluntariness which matches exactly a forward reference in the *EE*: there is no such matching reference in the *NE*.

Similarly, in the account of purposive choice the *EE* looks

M

forward to the *AE* treatment to a much greater extent than the *NE* does. The *EE* discusses the relationship of virtue to continence, the relationship of virtue to ends and means, the distinction between virtue and wisdom: all of them topics which are to be taken up and developed in precisely similar terminology in *AE* ʙ and ᴄ. The *EE* treatment gives us hints, which the *NE* does not, how we are to relate the early account of technical deliberation with the account of ethical deliberation developed in the *AE*.

Finally, in the treatment of practical reasoning, while the contribution of the *AE* far surpasses those of either the *NE* or the *EE*, it is the *EE* which offers a number of precisions which prepare the way for the full *AE* treatment. Thus, to take just two instances, it is the *EE* and not the *NE* which introduces the distinction between the possession and the exercise of knowledge which is fundamental to Aristotle's solution of the problem of ἀκρασία in *AE* ᴄ; and it is the *EE* and not the *NE* which works out in complete detail the sense in which the acts of the incontinent are voluntary—a point which is fundamental to the right understanding of the problem which *AE* ᴄ sets out to solve.

A consideration of Aristotle's treatment of the will, therefore, confirms the evidence from history, from style, and from other philosophical considerations to the conclusion that the common books of the *AE* had their original home in the *Eudemian* and not in the *Nicomachean Ethics*.

Can we draw any further conclusions about the relative chronology of Aristotle's ethical writings? It is often argued that the *Nicomachean Ethics* must be later than the *Eudemian* on the grounds that it exhibits a greater degree of sophistication and must therefore be the work of a more mature philosopher.

On the topics covered by the present study the most sophisticated passages to be found in Aristotle are probably those in the *AE* itself; so that the question of the comparative sophistication of the *NE* and the *EE* cannot altogether be separated from the question of the domicile of the common books. If we leave this question on one side for a moment, what conclusions are suggested by a comparison between the *NE* and *EE* considered in isolation?

It seems to me that though each of the treatises has merits and demerits not shared by the other, so far as concerns the treatment of the will the *EE* is on balance the philosophically more sophisticated of the two. This again can be illustrated by considering the three topics of the present work in turn.

The *NE* theory of the relation of remorse to voluntariness is generally regarded by commentators as a blot upon the book in which it occurs: the *EE* is better off without it. The *NE*, as we have seen, exhibits a confusion on the topic of συγγνώμη (pardon or excuse) which it is not easy to unravel. On the topic of crimes of passion the *EE* is clearer as well as more lenient than the *NE*; on the topic of duress both treatises are obscure, but the *EE* has the merit of raising the important question of the voluntariness of the duress itself as a factor relevant to acts performed under duress. The *EE* introduces useful philosophical distinctions (such as the one between relevant and irrelevant knowledge) which are absent from the *NE*.

The *EE* treatment of voluntariness is both fuller and more systematic than the *NE* treatment. It is more systematic in itself: it motivates the transitions from one topic to another much more clearly, while the *NE* is a collection of ill-connected jottings including a number of doublets. It is much more closely linked to the development of topics within the *Ethics*, as well as being much more related to Aristotle's general physical theory of causation and change. It contains passages of undoubted obscurity, and arguments of very doubtful validity: the key to the right appreciation of these is to be found in a fuller realisation of the nature of dialectical argument in Aristotle, of which the treatment of incontinence in *AE* c is generally, and rightly, regarded as providing a paradigm example. While much remains obscure in the *EE*, we may hope that when it has been studied as long and as lovingly as the *NE* it will be at least as clear. There have, after all, been no more than three or four commentaries on the *EE* in all history, while for centuries the *NE* has been commented on about once a decade.

The *EE* treatment of προαίρεσις is much fuller than the *NE* treatment: one could make much better sense of the *EE* concept if the *EE* stood alone than one could of the *NE* concept without the aid of the *AE*. Commentators have long been aware of a tension between the account of deliberation in the *NE* and in the *AE*: indeed, as I have argued, they have exaggerated it. The tension would have been much less, and the tendency to exaggerate it would have been minimal, if the *AE* had been studied in the context of the *EE* rather than of the *NE*.

On the topic of practical reasoning, as I have observed, neither the *NE* nor the *EE* can do much more than throw some sidelong light on the much fuller treatment of the topic in the *AE*. But the *EE* develops at much greater and more illuminating length the medical analogy with ethical inference and the parallel between the premises of theoretical reasoning and those of practical reasoning. But there are valuable items in the *NE* (such as the consideration of the possibility of exploring blind alleys in deliberation, and the division of means into instruments and actions) which are absent from the *EE*.[1]

The comparison we have made between the *NE* and the *EE* gives no support, it seems to me, to the claim that the *NE* must be later than the *EE* because it is more sophisticated. An attempt to base a chronological claim on a judgment about comparative philosophical sophistication seems to me always a risky matter. But if any such claim were to be made in the present instance it would, it seems to me, have to be a claim for the posteriority of the *EE*, not of the *NE*.

If I am right in thinking that the *AE* fits the *EE* context better than it fits the *NE* context, and that where the *NE* and the *EE* differ it is the latter which is the more sophisticated,

---

[1] I have not given any extended consideration in this work to the question of the voluntariness of states of character (ἕξεις) as opposed to the voluntariness of character: a topic which is discussed in *NE* 3.5. Though this is an interesting and relevant topic, I have avoided it for two reasons. First, an adequate treatment of it would have involved discussion of determinism and Aristotle's attitude to it; and though I believe (see Kenny, 1975, *passim*) that determinism is irrelevant to questions of the freedom of the will, and though I believe Aristotle would have shared this view, this belief takes considerable argument to justify which would have swollen the present monograph excessively. Secondly, a comparison with the corresponding part of the *EE* (the treatment of luck and virtue in *EE* viii) would have involved a difficult effort of textual criticism in the reconstruction of a text generally regarded as extremely corrupt.

then it follows that reading the *EE* and the *AE* together, i.e. the traditional *Eudemian Ethics*, will be a more rewarding philosophical exercise than reading the *NE* and the *AE* together, i.e. the traditional *Nicomachean Ethics*. Aristotle's theory of the will, I have claimed, has still a great deal of light to throw on the difficult problems in this area: it will throw a great deal more when we become as accustomed to reading the common books in their Eudemian context as we have been for centuries to reading them in a Nicomachean context.

BIBLIOGRAPHY

ALLAN, D. J. 'The Practical Syllogism', in *Autour d'Aristote*, Louvain 1955.

ANSCOMBE, G. E. M. *Intention*, Oxford 1957.

'Thought and Action in Aristotle', in Barnes, Schofield and Sorabji 1977, 76–71.

ANDO, T. *Aristotle's Theory of Practical Cognition*, Kyoto 1958.

AUBENQUE, P. 'La Prudence aristotélicienne, porte-t-elle sur la fin ou sur les moyens?', *Revue des Etudes Grecques* 78 (1965), 40–51.

BARNES, J., SCHOFIELD, M., and SORABJI, R., *Articles on Aristotle 2: Ethics*, London 1977.

COOPER, J. M. *Reason and Human Good in Aristotle*, London 1975.

DIRLMEIER, F. *Aristoteles, Magna Moralia, übersetzt und erlautert*, Berlin 1958.

Aristotles, Nikomakische Ethik, übersetzt und kommentiert, Berlin 1959.

Aristoteles, Eudemische Ethik, übersetzt und kommentiert, Berlin 1969.

FORTENBAUGH, W. W. '*Ta pros to telos* and Syllogistic Vocabulary in Aristotle's Ethics', *Phronesis* 10 (1965), 191–201.

FRAGSTEIN, A. von, *Die Diairesis bei Aristoteles*, Amsterdam 1967.

Studien zur Ethik des Aristoteles, Amsterdam 1974.

FRITZSCHE, A. T. H. *Eudemi Rhodi Ethica*, Regensburg 1851.

FURLEY, D. J. 'Aristotle on the Voluntary', in Barnes, Schofield and Sorabji 1977, 47–60.

GAUTHIER, D. *Practical Reasoning*, Ithaca 1961.

GAUTHIER, R. A. and JOLIF, J. Y. *L'Ethique à Nicomaque*, Louvain 1958 and 1959.

GAUTHIER, R. A. Introduction to second edition of *L'Ethique à Nicomaque*, Louvain 1959.

GREENWOOD, L. H. G. *Aristotle, Nicomachean Ethics Book VI*, Cambridge 1909.

HARDIE, W. F. R. *Aristotle's Ethical Theory*, Oxford 1968.

JACKSON, H. *The Fifth Book of the Nicomachean Ethics of Aristotle*, Cambridge 1879.

KENNY, A. *Action, Emotion and Will*, London 1963.

'The Practical Syllogism and Incontinence', *Phronesis* 11 (1966), 163–84.

Will, Freedom and Power, London 1975.

The Aristotelian Ethics, Oxford 1978.

MONAN, J. D. *Moral Knowledge and its Methodology in Aristotle*, Oxford 1968.

OSTWALD, M. *Aristotle, Nicomachean Ethics, translated with introduction and notes*, Indianapolis 1962.

RACKHAM, H. *The Eudemian Ethics* (Loeb edition), London 1935.

ROSS, W. D. *Aristotle*, London 1949.
The Works of Aristotle, vol ix, Oxford 1925.

ROWE, C., *The Eudemian and Nicomachean Ethics*, Cambridge 1971.

SCHOFIELD, M. 'Aristotelian Mistakes', *Proceedings of the Cambridge Philological Society*, 19 (1973), 66–70.

SOLOMON, J. 'Translation of the Eudemian Ethics', *The Oxford Aristotle* ix, Oxford 1925.

WALTER, J. *Die Lehre von der praktischen Vernunft in der griechischen Philosophie*, Jena 1864.

WALZER, R. *Magna Moralia and Aristotelische Ethik*, Berlin 1929.

WIGGINS, D. 'Deliberation and Practical Reason', *Proceedinge of the Aristotelian Society* 76 (1935/6), 29–51.

INDEX OF ARISTOTELIAN PASSAGES

INDEX OF MODERN AUTHORS

INDEX OF SUBJECTS